Henry Joseph Pflugbeil

St. Thomas Manual

Henry Joseph Pflugbeil

St. Thomas Manual

ISBN/EAN: 9783337395551

Printed in Europe, USA, Canada, Australia, Japan

Cover: Foto ©Lupo / pixelio.de

More available books at **www.hansebooks.com**

ST. THOMAS MANUAL:

OR

Devotion of the Six Sundays in Honor

OF THE

ANGEL OF THE SCHOOLS,

ST. THOMAS OF AQUIN.

From the German of

Father Henry Joseph Pflugbeil, O. Pr.

'Behold, I will send my angel, who shall go before thee."
Exodus, XXIII. 20.

FR. PUSTET,
Printer to the Holy See, and the S. Congregation of Rites.

FR. PUSTET & CO.
NEW YORK AND CINCINNATI.

PREFACE.

"Non est inventus similis illi!"—If, as some writer has said, "Unrest is the characteristic of our age," is it less true to affirm that our craving after knowledge is not confined exclusively to the profane sciences? In the domain of literature we find many turning from the vague, insipid writings of the day to the more solid intellectual food of mediæval times. And nowhere is this more apparent than in our devotions. The old and familiar "Six Sundays" of the youthful Aloysius, the June devotion of all Catholic schools and colleges, are now to be yearly preceded by those of the "Angel of the Schools."

As St. Thomas Aquinas is held to be *par excellence* the great theologian of the Catholic Church, nay, even the Doctor by whom her later Doctors were guided in their writings, we are safe in yielding to the impulse to choose him for our special patron of science and study. And could we better show our earnestness as clients than by meditating on his life, his virtues, his own mode of study, and the motives that actuated every thought of his vast mind, every movement of his noble heart?

The precious little volume before us is destined to do a big work in its English costume. It has been translated for all that wish to warm their heart in the rays of this great, theological sun; for all that desire to enjoy the special protection and intercession of the saint; for all that would find a practical aid in their devotion.

The "Six Sundays" of St. Thomas, properly made, cannot fail, in colleges especially, to recruit the army of the Lord. Our youth will be inspirited by the example of so valiant a champion to follow in his footsteps and make piety the foundation of learning.

Who, upon reading the story of St. Thomas's investiture with the Holy Girdle, would not ambition enrolment in the "Angelic Militia," of which he is the noble leader? Who would not aspire to gird themselves with his Cord to which are annexed so many powerful auxiliaries for the combat, so many rewards for the victory?

The Hymns and Prayers of the Angelic Doctor, the Daily Devotions of Father von Cochem at the end of the little book, are treasures of piety well calculated to stir up devotion in the coldest heart and quicken the fervor of the most devout. May this gem of Manuals find a place in every school and college and household of our broad, fair land, and may saints be multiplied by its use!

DEDICATION.

He whom thou didst so purely and religiously serve,

O marvellous Angel of the Schools,

ST. THOMAS OF AQUIN,

did not despise the widow's mite, because He "considers the heart and not the gift." And do thou accept this token from one that has nothing better to offer, but whose grateful soul must make some return for the protection thou hast ever accorded him. O that, in accordance with the wish of our Holy Father, Leo XIII., who has appointed thee the special patron of Catholic students, and in the sentiments of all the Popes that have recommended thee to veneration as the protector of innocence, I could place numbers under thy trusty guidance through the struggles of youth and the dangers that menace its innocence! There would then be many to express their gratitude better than I, many to undertake greater things for thy honor; but may no one surpass me, thy poor client, in grateful sentiments and faithful love!

INTRODUCTION.

OUR Holy Father, Pope Leo XIII., gloriously reigning, following the example of so many of his illustrious predecessors, has repeatedly proclaimed the praises of St. Thomas of Aquin and enthusiastically recommended his veneration. If Pope John XXII., on the occasion of the saint's canonization, expressed himself thus: "He has wrought as many miracles as he has written articles;" if Innocent VI. has said: "No one that holds to his teaching, can ever wander from the path of truth ; but he that attacks him has always been suspected of error;" if other successors of the Prince of the Apostles declare of the Angelic Doctor: "His writings are without error, and he himself is the most glorious champion of the Catholic faith,"—Pope Leo XIII. has repeated the eulogiums of his predecessors and added to them.

In his Encyclical of August 4, 1879, to the Bishops of the Catholic world upon the revival of Christian Philosophy in Catholic schools according to the spirit of the Angelic Teacher, Thomas of Aquin, he says: "Among scholastic teachers, ranks above all as prince and master Thomas of Aquin, who honored in the highest degree the saintly teachers of the early Church whose spirit he had imbibed. Thomas gathered together and united their teachings, like scattered members of the human frame, set them in order with wondrous skill, developed and augmented them so considerably that with perfect right is he esteemed the most illustrious support of the Catholic Church. Of a mind logical and penetrating; a memory quick and retentive; above all, a life pure and tending to God alone; rich in knowledge human and divine, he has like the sun vivified the world by the light of his virtues, and filled it with the splendor of his doctrines."

Not satisfied with the foregoing encomiums, the Vicar of Jesus Christ one year later, in a Decree of August 8, 1880, declared St. Thomas of Aquin the patron of all Catholic schools. On this occasion, the Holy Father added the following words to the praises already bestowed:—"The Angelic Doctor," he says among other things, "is as exalted in virtue and holiness as in erudition. He may be compared to the angelic spirits not less on account of his innocence, than on account of his endowments."

Through such commendations, and still more through the choice made of St. Thomas as patron of Catholic schools, the desire arose to obtain new Indulgences for the devotion of the new, saintly protector. Upon the presentation of this petition, His Holiness granted to the Devotion of the Six Sundays either before or after the feast of St. Thomas of Aquin, March 7th, the same Indulgences as were accorded by his predecessors to the Six Sundays of St. Aloysius.

The petition for the above ran thus :—

MOST HOLY FATHER!

Humbly prostrate at the feet of your Holiness, I, Father Marcolinus Cicognani, Procurator-General of the Dominican Order, to express the wishes of numerous members of the same, also to increase the devotion and attachment of the faithful, and especially of students for their holy and angelic protector St. Thomas of Aquin, beg that all, who, on each of the six consecutive Sundays that precede or follow the feast of the Angelic Doctor, St. Thomas of Aquin, confess with true contrition, receive Holy Communion, make the considerations, recite the pious prayers, and devoutly perform other religious exercises, may gain a Plenary Indulgence on each of the Six Sundays (applicable to the souls in purgatory) similar to those accorded by the Roman Pontiffs to the Sundays of St. Aloysius of Gonzaga.

ANSWER OF THE HOLY CONGREGATION OF INDULGENCES.

Our Holy Father, Pope Leo XIII., has in the audience that the undersigned deputy of the Secretary of the Holy Congregation of Indulgences and Relics had on the 21st of August, 1886, most graciously granted the request, the said grant to remain in force without the expediting of a Brief, nothing to the contrary notwithstanding, etc.

Given at Rome in the Secretary's Office of the Holy Congregation, August 21, 1886.

(L. S.)   J. B. CARDINAL FRANZELIN, Prefect,
   JOSEPHUS M. CANONICUS COSELLI, Deputy.

The Indulgences for the Sundays of St. Aloysius are, according to Father Haringer ("Spiritual Treasury," Authorized Edition, Ratisbon—Manz 1878) as follows:

Pope Clement XII. in two Decrees of the Holy Congregation of Indulgences, dated Dec. 11, 1739 and Jan. 7, 1760, granted a Plenary Indulgence on each of the Six Sundays kept in honor of St. Aloysius Gonzaga, either consecutively before his feast or at any other time during the year. But in order to gain these Indulgences, it is requisite that the Six Sundays should be kept consecutively, and that the faithful on each, being truly penitent and having communicated, should make use of some pious considerations or vocal prayers or other works of Christian piety in honor of the saint.

As the feast of St. Thomas of Aquin is celebrated in the Dominican Order as a feast of the First Class, March the 7th, the Six Sundays in his honor begin at the earliest on the 24th of January and at the latest on January the 30th, as shown below:—

In case the 7th of March falls upon a

Day	1st Sunday falls on	(Leap-Year)
Sunday,	24th of Jan.	25th
Monday,	30th	31st
Tuesday,	29th	30th
Wednesday,	28th	29th
Thursday,	27th	28th
Friday,	26th	27th
Saturday,	25th	26th

As for gaining the Indulgences pious exercises are prescribed as a condition, the following considerations are now offered to facilitate the efforts of the faithful. He who feels devotion aroused by one point of the Consideration for each Sunday, would do well to pause upon it, and leave the rest for spiritual reading at some other hour during the day.

May the Angelic Doctor, by means of this little book, assist many souls to join the choirs of the angels! Then will be fulfilled this sentence of the title-page: "Behold I will send my angel, who shall go before thee." (Exodus XXIII, 20.)

VENLO, Ash-Wednesday, 1887.

CONSIDERATIONS

FOR THE

Six Sundays in Honor of the Angelic Doctor,
ST. THOMAS OF AQUIN.

CONSIDERATION FOR THE FIRST SUNDAY.

St. Thomas's Early Yearnings after God.

> "*Solus Deus voluntatem hominis implere potest.... In solo igitur Deo beatitudo hominis consistit,*"
>
> (St. Thom. Summa Theol. I. 2 qu. II. a. 8.)
>
> "God alone can fill the heart of man.... Therefore in God alone man's happiness consists."

FIRST POINT.—Consider first, that St. Thomas even from the dawn of reason tended with his whole soul to God. As a boy of five years, he was entrusted to the Benedictines of Monte Cassino. Scarcely arrived at self-consciousness, Thomas already sought by his questions some knowledge of God; or, as his first biographer expresses it, "impelled by divine instinct, he longed to hear of God." The great theologian who was to throw such light on the mysteries of God as none before or after him has ever done, early began his search after what was to be the aim of his whole life, the radiant centre of his knowledge. How touching for those sons of St. Benedict, men grown old in communing with God, when in the midst of the games and childlike prattle of the other boys, the future Angel of the Schools, then only five years old, raising his innocent eyes to theirs, would gravely and reverently ask: "What is God?"—And though answered again and again that God is what human tongue cannot express nor angelic intelligence comprehend, he never desisted from repeating: "What is God?"—a question that the monks of Monte Cassino were unable to answer, and that even now in the light of glory they find incomprehensible. It was the brilliant sun upon which the mental eye of the great St. Thomas unweariedly gazed.

The more puzzled the teachers became at his devout question, "What is God?"—the clearer did that very fact make it appear to the boy that God alone, in His incomprehensible beauty and perfection, deserves to be known and loved above all things. What the pure soul of the boy, attracted by the Creator and prevented by the grace of the Redeemer, irresistibly sought, was to him all the dearer on account of the infinitely surpassing greatness of the Supreme Good. He felt what long before St. Ephrem had expressed: "He is hidden from thee, O seeker, though readily disclosed to thy adoration!"

But what is adoration? Nothing else than entire submission, perfect resignation.

Now, ask thyself, O my soul, whether at the moment of thy arrival at self-conciousness, God alone became thy highest aim and end. When didst thou begin to refer thy whole life to Him, to seek Him everywhere, to behold him in all things? When reason dawns, our actions, as emanating from a self-conscious being, become accountable; hence, they must tend to our last end, and according to the same be regulated. Every thought, every word, every action in harmonious accord with God, is good, leads to God, and merits a reward; whilst the contrary is repelled by His infinite sanctity, and loads the responsible agent with guilt. Either one or the other is the consequence of every act of the free-will. This undeniable truth stamps the value upon all our actions, influences our whole life, and consequently determines our fate for eternity. And yet, the unthinking world heedless of this truth runs on, it cares not whither. If after thy self-examen, thou discoverest that thou, too, hast frittered away thy life unmindful of thy destiny and that of the things around thee, transport thyself in spirit to those early days on Monte Cassino, and listen humbly to the earnest question of Thomas, a boy of five years: "What is God?" Let the innocent accents of the future *Doctor Angelicus* sink deep into thy soul and find therein the echo, "What is God!"—Is He not thy end and aim? Did He not create thee for Himself? Has He not a right over thee? Has He not almighty power over thee? Canst thou escape Him? If thou fleest from Him, wilt thou not like the Prophet Jonas rush into the arms of thy angry God?

What, then, must thou do? O happy for thee if only a short space of thy life has been spent so inconsiderately! Happier still if the retrospect unfolds to thee no misspent, no valueless existence! Have thy lost hours been few? Then let mingled sorrow and joy temper the ardor with which thou wilt now hasten to consecrate to God every moment left to thee, and thus consecrating it secure it for thyself.—If, however, the greater part of thy life is already wasted—Ah, then, with still greater ardor press onward ere it is too late! Had a tepid religious of Monte Cassino, or a worldling tarrying there awhile, heard the innocent child lovingly and earnestly asking: "What is God?"—would it not have struck upon his soul like a lightning flash? Would it not have filled him with deepest shame and self-reproach? Yes, unquestionably, those words must have burned into the most callous heart. And so may they burn into thine! May a ray from the clear eyes of that angelic child pierce thy heart, and to his question, "What is God?"—give to him and to thyself the answer: "God is what no one heretofore could be to me, what no one in the future can be: my last end, my highest aim."

Second Point.—Consider how St. Thomas of Aquin during his whole life kept this aim before his eyes, all others being secondary thereto. "Impossible!" does he exclaim, "Impossible to find happiness in a created good, for the state of blessedness exacts that all longing should cease! That which leaves something still to strive after, can never be the highest aim; consequently, nothing can satisfy the heart of man but that good which contains in itself and of itself all good. Now, that Good is God alone. Creatures possess but a good received ; God is in Himself all good."

So taught the wise master, and his life was in accord with his teachings. Once arrived at the conviction that the goods of earth could not satisfy his heart created for eternal bliss, it cost him no struggle to put them aside for the Supreme Good. The wealthy, young nobleman, sprung from the blood of the Norman princes, closely allied to the imperial House of Hohenstaufen, with the most magnificent future opening up before him, to the dismay of his teachers, to the sorrow of his otherwise pious mother, to the indignation of his brothers and the astonishment of the world at large, took the resolution to enter the poor and but recently founded Dominican Order. He overcame all obstacles, and like a hero struggled for the coveted happiness of becoming a mendicant friar. All the allurements of a later period, intercourse with kings and rulers, with cardinals and with Popes—all that his high position in the world could bestow, made no impression on the saintly youth who knew so well that our happiness consists in God alone.

Now dost thou begin, O Christian soul, to realize the practice of these words: "To recognize God as the supreme end, and for him alone to live."

Thou mayest already have chosen thy state in life, or thou mayest be about to make that choice, or peradventure thou mayest still much longer ponder over the same. In any case, God's will should ever be thy rule of conduct, the only consideration which should influence thy decision. As soon as thou preferest a creature to God, as soon as thou ceasest to weigh thy actions by their reference to God, canst thou be sure that thou art laboring at thine own eternal happiness? Since the creature can give no lasting felicity and thou art at war with the true Source of joy, whence shalt thou find peace?

Study well, then, by what way thou, with thy talents, thy abilities, thy peculiar graces, canst most safely and surely arrive at union with God, at that state of purity in which thou wilt find God; or if thou hast already chosen a permanent state in life, then consider how thou mayest best put thy affairs with God in order. It is neither necessary nor possible for all to follow St. Thomas to the cloister. For that a special vocation from God would be demanded. But it is not only necessary but indispensable that we should all follow him in the way that leads to God; that like him we should make God our chief aim; that all other aims in life should be subservient thereto; and that the goods, the joys, the delights of this earth should exert upon us only so much influence as may promote our striving after God. If our trust is placed in God alone, the words of the Psalmist shall never be verified in us; "They that go far from Thee shall perish." (Ps. LXXII, 27.)

Cast an earnest glance upon thy angelic leader on this the first of his Six Sundays, and by a thorough examination of thy soul, see whether all in thee tends to the Lord, thy God, whether there is aught in thee displeasing in His sight. What is there in thy heart that can attract upon thee His approving gaze, or what is there that must be cast out in order to please Him? What means must thou take to discover in what vocation God's grace will best be preserved to thee?—or if thy vocation be already decided, what is there in it that does not lead thee to God?—what is there that must absolutely be abandoned?

Think not that it is so very difficult to relinquish earthly goods for the Supreme Good. How many thousands have learned by experience that the very disengaging of the heart from the burden of temporal attachments, brings with it its own reward, and that in freedom of soul lies an indemnification far outweighing the joys of earth!—The severing of the affections from everything that could separate the soul from God, is what must take place under all circumstances whatsoever.

Since God has in Himself all good, thou canst lose nothing even in the supposition that thou art called upon to sacrifice all for Him. In Him all will be restored to thee; and, moreover, thou wilt find in Him what out of Him thou canst nowhere meet.

Rejoice that even now at the beginning, the Angelic Master incites thee to aims so high, and exacts so much of thee. He who sets such a price upon the good he offers, must be thoroughly convinced of its immeasurable value. St. Thomas, here as everywhere, is in strict harmony with Eternal Truth which says: "The kingdom of heaven is like to a merchant seeking good pearls. Who when he had found one pearl of great price, went his way, and sold all that he had, and bought it."

Prayer.

O Angelic Teacher, St. Thomas of Aquin, thou didst early begin to seek that which alone is worth the efforts of an immortal spirit! That thou wast permitted to gaze so far into the abyss of God's infinite perfections, is no marvel to me; since even in thy childhood thou didst, like a young eagle fix thine eyes upon the radiance of His divine splendor. O how happy should I be if like thee my early affections had all been given to God, and again like thee I had been true to my first love! And yet even now I may count myself happy if, under thy guidance, I run on unshackled by the things of earth and, at last, reach the Supreme Good. Nothing, nothing shall now impede my progress. If my state in life forbids the absolute resignation of exterior things, it cannot prevent the entire detachment of my heart from them. Exultingly as the lark on a summer morn, shall my heart soar up to God, to breathe the pure air whence thou didst draw such abundance of grace, and near thee to learn how pitiful is all that is not God.

Obtain for me the grace, O my angelic guide, to love God above all things, not merely in word, but in heart and in deed. I am sincerely resolved to live for Him, to die for Him. But I know my weakness to be such that without heavenly assistance my resolve can produce no lasting effects. Ah then, be thou my special protector and guide on the way to God? Obtain that like thee, my saintly model, I may sigh for no other reward in the toils of this life than God alone for all eternity! Amen.

Prayer of the Church for the Feast of St. Thomas of Aquin.

(To be repeated after every Consideration.)

O God, who by the wonderful learning of blessed Thomas, Thy confessor, hast illustrated Thy Church, and by his virtues hast enlarged it: grant, we beseech Thee, that we may understand what he taught and in our lives follow what he practised. Through Christ, our Lord. Amen.

Trait from the Life of St. Thomas of Aquin.

Whilst St. Thomas was sojourning in the Monastery at Naples, there appeared to him once when praying in the church, Brother Romanus, whom he had left in Paris as Master of Theology. Thomas addressed him as follows: "Welcome! When did you arrive?"—to which the apparition answered: "I have passed from this life; but I have been permitted to appear to you for your own good."— For a moment overcome by the sight of his deceased friend, St. Thomas quickly collected himself and said: "If it be pleasing to God, I intreat you in His name to answer these questions: How do I stand? Does my life please God?"—"You are in a good state and your works are pleasing to God," was the reply. Then the holy Master went on: "How is it with yourself?" "I am in eternal life," answered the deceased, "though I was for sixteen days in purgatory, on account of my tardiness in carrying into effect a will intrusted to me by the Bishop of Paris."—"Tell me," inquired Thomas, "how is it with that question we so often discussed, whether in the other life the soul remains in the particular state acquired in this?"—"Brother Thomas," answered the apparition, "I see God! Ask nothing more."—"But," rejoined the saint, "in what way do you see God? Do you see Him immediately, or by means of some image?" —Then replied the spirit: "As we have heard so have we seen in the city of the Lord of Hosts!" —and vanished, leaving the holy Master filled with joy and astonishment.

It was likewise in the Monastery of Naples that happened the well-known incident, so often represented in pictures, and which serves as another proof that the first thought of the great Master was God. The sacristan, Brother Dominic of Caserta, a man of acknowledged virtue joined to prayer and labor, had frequently remarked that Thomas was in the habit of leaving his cell before Matins to go to the church, whence he afterwards hurried back as if wishing to be seen by none. This led to closer observation on the part of Brother Dominic. He entered the Chapel of St. Nicolas as the saint knelt there in prayer, and saw him, rapt in ecstasy, raised two cubits in the air.

Whilst the Brother gazed in awe and astonishment, he distinctly heard the following words addressed to the saint from the Crucifix: "Well hast thou written of Me, Thomas! What reward wilt thou accept for thy labor?"—To which Thomas at once answered: "No other than Thyself, O Lord!"— "Justly," continues the narrator, "did he desire for reward in the heavenly country Him in whom, by his labor upon earth, he had already found so much joy."

And happy wilt thou be, my friend, if thou hast the assurance, not from a departed soul, but from thy own conscience, from God Himself, that thy life is pleasing to Him, that thy works can stand the test of His all-seeing eye! And more blessed still wilt thou be if, like the great St. Thomas: thou desirest God alone for thy reward!

CONSIDERATION FOR THE SECOND SUNDAY.

St. Thomas' Love of Chastity. His Great Temptation.

FIRST POINT.—Consider St. Thomas coming off unscathed from the frightful temptation to which his chastity was exposed. He had in peace of soul resisted the temptations of an effeminate, luxurious city and those in particular that beset a university life. He was like an angel among beastly and diabolical slaves of vice. No shadow ever fell upon his virtue, no breath of sensuality ever tarnished the pure mirror of his soul. But lo! from a quarter whence it was least to be expected, from those that should have admired and protected his innocence, came the danger. His resolution to enter the Dominican Order had filled his mother's heart with sorrow, his brothers' with indignation; and the otherwise pious mother approved a step from which, under other circumstances, she would have turned in horror. Thomas's brothers had learned in the army of the Emperor Frederic II. to look lightly upon any measure deemed expedient by them, to crush whatever militated against their pride of birth. In pursuance of their object, they unexpectedly attacked the young novice when on his way to Paris, took him prisoner, and led him to their castle of Rocca Sicca where he was treated as a malefactor. He was imprisoned in one of the towers and no one allowed to approach him excepting his sisters, who were commissioned to dissuade him from his stupid intention of becoming a mendicant friar. But when the contrary happened and the two girls turned from worldly amusements, to become the champions of their noble brother and zealous servants of God; when every species of violence proved fruitless, then did the brothers adopt the diabolical resolution to rob the angelical youth of his purity and with it of divine grace. As with Samson in the arms of Dalila, so should it be with our young hero—the secret of his heavenly strength and virtue would be betrayed and the victory over him won. "They thought," says his first biographer, "to conquer him by other tactics—tactics by which strong towers have been shaken, hard rocks softened, and the cedars of Libanus uprooted in the storm. The struggle was to be that in which there are, indeed, many combatants but few victors." During the night, a charming, but sinful girl in immodest attire, was introduced into the chamber of the holy youth for the purpose of tempting him to sin. But the hero of God, his heart glowing with love for Divine Wisdom, his chosen bride, had scarcely remarked the threatening danger, and knowing that flight, the best remedy on such occasions, was prohibited him, when seizing a blazing brand from the hearth, he drove the vile wretch from the room. Then, burning with holy enthusiasm, he ran to a corner of his chamber, drew with his charred weapon a cross on the wall, and cast himself on his knees before it in an ecstasy of prayer, begging Almighty God to preserve to him ever what His grace had enabled him to bring from the combat unscathed.

With feelings of wonder and admiration, gaze in spirit upon that champion of virginity coming forth from the contest in which many struggle, but few bear off the palm. Shall I call thee happy if still ignorant of the dangers attendant on such strifes? or happier if thou hast already fought and conquered? But blessed is he that has chosen such a leader as St. Thomas! Think not that trials similar to his will be spared thee. It may not, perhaps, be thy brethren who will lay for thee the snare—though in this very point the words of the Lord are too often verified: "A man's enemies are those of his own household." The peculiar circumstances of each one's life are somewhat different from those of his neighbor, as are also the dangers consequent on the same; but for none are they wanting, and for all in the main point they are very similar: human frailty on the one hand, the allurements of pleasure on the other. Wilt thou be stronger than the many that, confiding in self, miserably fell? Will it not be better for thee to imitate thy angelic guide and daily before the Crucifix, whence virginity first derived its value since the Son of the Virgin hung thereon, implore God's help? "As I knew," says Solomon, "That I could not otherwise be continent except God gave it, and this also was a point of wisdom, to know whose gift it was: I went to the Lord and besought Him, and said with my whole heart: "God of my fathers and Lord of mercy, ... give me wisdom that sitteth by thy throne, and cast me not off from among thy children, for I am thy servant and the son of thy hand-maid, a weak man." (Wis. VIII, 21; IX, 1, 4, 5.) The cross is the throne whereon hung the Incarnate Wisdom, and whence strength flows to preserve body and soul chaste. O treasure highly this virtue which, in His last bequest upon the cross, Our Lord especially provided for when He commended the Virgin Mother to the Virgin disciple! On the cross it hangs, and by the cross it lives. If the enemy draws near, seize this fiery weapon, love for the Crucified. Hold thyself in readiness, for thou knowest not the moment of his approach. Fire in this case must be extinguished by fire. But think not to conquer if thou dost neglect to enkindle within thee the fire of divine love, if thou dost defer until the hellish seduction glares upon thee or the enemy has roused up thy evil passions. The pure flame of God's love must burn brightly, that thou mayest resist the foul fires of Satan.

SECOND POINT.—As St. Thomas was praying after his victory, he fell into an ecstasy. A throng of angels surrounded him, and two of them bound his loins with the girdle of continence saying: "Commissioned by God, we came to bring thee the gift of perpetual virginity, which irrevocable grace He now insures to thee."—The pain of this binding roused him and drew from him an involuntary cry. On hearing it, his guards entered the room; but he carefully hid his secret from them, and spoke not of it until his death. Notwithstanding the assurance that he would always preserve his chastity, Thomas was prudent and watchful as before. He fled all company and, especially, conversation with females. His reserve on this point was so remarkable that it aroused some dissatisfaction on the part of those thus shunned. Once a noble lady asked him in complaining, though respectful tones, why he so studiously kept aloof from speech with women, since he had himself been born of a woman. To which the clear-sighted and circumspect Master answered: "I shun women for the very reason that I myself was born of a woman."—By which words he meant to say that, knowing himself to be a weak child of Adam, he looked upon such caution as necessary. It was by such circumspection that he maintained his purity so unsullied that his friend, Brother Reginald a Piperno, to whom more than once he had made a general confession, deposed upon oath after the saint's death that his innocence was such as to render the last confession of his life like that of a boy of five years.

He that would quietly observe the deportment of most men, noticing how coolly they abandon themselves to danger, might be tempted to conclude that peril had vanished from earth, or that man had become inaccessible to evil. Where is he to be found who has not some weak point? Who has not heard of the Grecian hero Achilles whose mother dipped him in dragon's blood, in order to render him invulnerable? But the heel by which she held him not coming in contact with the charmed bath, did not share in the virtue communicated to the rest of his person; and it was in that very heel that Achilles received the fatal wound which brought him death. Now, this weak point, this heel of Achilles, may likewise be found in thee. If strong in other points, thou art, owing to the sin of our first parents, in matters relating to the delicate, holy virtue, so weak and infirm that thou canst not promise thyself security without great watchfulness and the constant help of God. Art thou stronger than those mighty ones of earth, those courageous heros, those able warriors, those wise and holy ones who, in an unguarded moment, fell to such depths that for nearly three thousand years the wailing notes of the "Miserere" have risen from the imitators of him whose own sad fall called that cry for mercy into being? If the cedars of Libanus, the strong towers of mighty citadels could not withstand such whirlwinds, be thou now fearful that later on thou mayest not have to mourn and do penance. If he whom angels bound with the cincture of chastity; whom they thereby admitted to their own number; yes, to whom, in the name of God, they expressly declared the gift of virginity secured,—if St. Thomas, notwithstanding all this was so cautious, with how much greater reason is the most rigorous circumspection needful to thee? "Sensual pleasure," says the holy Doctor, "more than all things else weakens the strength of the soul. The spiritual eye grows blind, the will becomes lame, as soon as this horrible, this filthy passion gains ground." Be mindful! Every glance must be guarded, every motion, every thought kept under control, that the enemy may not steal into the heart and establish there his reign even before thou dreamest of the magnitude of the danger.

Hast thou in time past been thus conscientious? Had an improper word the power to offend thy chaste ear? a suspicious picture to startle thy chaste eye?—or are thy eye and thy ear no longer chaste? Dost thou listen willingly to that from which a modest ear should turn? Art thou attracted to what should cause thy modest cheek to blush?—O tremble for thy treasure! A single glance can paint upon thy soul pictures that a lifetime will not be able to efface, and which may be for thee the cause of repeated struggles. Though cheerful in thy intercourse with others, art thou discreet and reserved? In thy demonstrations of affection, dost thou not express thyself with too much liberty and tenderness? Such demonstrations may sully the pure lily of chastity, if they do not wholly destroy it. O be careful!—Must thou reproach thyself with having exposed or even with having altogether ruined thy precious treasure?—O fly to the Angelic Doctor! His girdle, his cord works most efficaciously through the blessing of the Church. The angelic virtue under the protection of the Angelic Doctor will grow dear to thy soul, its practice easy and fruitful of blessing; for where earthly passion has been extinguished, there will be enkindled the celestial flame of the seraphim, there will be bestowed the bright vision of the cherubim of which Jesus says: "Blessed are the pure of heart, for they shall see God."

Prayer.

O holy, innocent Master, thou leader of the host pure of soul, I now begin to understand what gained for thee the title, "Angel of the Schools." The eye of an angel must indeed be able to contemplate that which constitutes an angel's blessedness. Well didst thou understand that saying of the Holy Spirit: "Wisdom will not enter into a malicious soul, nor dwell in a body subject to sin." —Thou hast told me that the heart that gives itself up to sensuality, must be weak, bad, and subject to low instincts. I believe thee, and I will follow thy counsels. Never will I have aught to do with what might endanger the lovely, the precious purity of my soul. When the tempter suddenly appears, may I like thee in the hour of thy fiery and memorable victory, seize the flaming brand of holy love with which to put my enemy to flight! I solemnly promise thee, O my holy Leader, to flee from every shadow of danger, to be watchful in the choice of my books, my friends, my conversations, my recreations, yes, even in my food and drink as far as in me lies. But do thou, O heavenly Protector, obtain for me the divine assistance in those encounters from which so few come forth victorious. I will conquer, I must conquer! Protect me from whatever could wound purity in the least degree and keep me in the love of this beautiful virtue till the end, that I may belong to those who in heaven thank thee for thy guard over them and contribute to thy glory, O thou triumphant Leader and renowned Hero of virginity! Amen.

Prayer of the Church.
(Page 17.)

Trait from the Life of St. Thomas of Aquin.

The witnesses at St. Thomas's canonization mentioned in their deposition the opinion openly expressed at the time of the saint's death; viz., that he had lived *perfectly pure and chaste*, and that *he had carried to the grave the virginity with which he had come into the world.*

The following fact is worthy of remark: On August 4, 1319, in presence of the Archbishop and the members of the Commission of Inquiry assembled at Naples, for the purpose of collecting evidence in St. Thomas's case, Brother Anthony of Brescia, Priest of the Dominican Order, affirmed upon oath that he had from Brother Albert of Brescia, a man of great sanctity and professor at Brescia, who closely followed the teaching of St. Thomas, often heard the words: "Thomas is a saint!"—adding as if perfectly convinced of the truth of his statement: "I know, my dear Brother, that he is a great saint in heaven."—When he, the witness, with one of his companions, Brother Janinus, since deceased, had long besought the above-mentioned Brother Albert to tell them how he knew with so much certainty that Brother Thomas was a saint, Brother Albert spoke, as follows:—

"You know, my dear sons, that in every point I follow the teaching of the saintly Thomas, and often have I wondered, how he in so short a lifetime*) should have attained such holiness and knowledge. Reflecting upon this astonishing fact, I repeatedly implored God through the intercession of the most holy Virgin and St. Augustine, to show to me the glory of Brother Thomas. One day whilst prostrate before the altar of the Blessed Virgin, being fully conscious and having prayed long with abundant tears, two noble looking men appeared to me. They shone with light and mag-

---

*) St. Thomas of Aquin died in his 49th year.

nificence. One wore a mitre; the other was habited in the Dominican garb, on his head a crown of gold set with precious stones, and around his neck two chains, one of gold, the other of silver. On his breast glittered a large magnificent jewel, whose radiance lit up the whole church. His cappa**) was covered with precious stones; his tunic***) and scapular radiated light as white as snow. Astounded at the wonderful vision, I cast myself at their feet and begged them to make known to me who they were in their glorious beauty. Thereupon he that wore the mitre answered: "Why art thou so amazed Brother Albert? Thy prayers have been heard. Behold, I now disclose to thee who we are! I am Augustine, the Doctor of the Church. I have been sent to thee in order to show the glory of Brother Thomas of Aquin, who here stands beside me. He is my son, inasmuch as he followed in all things the teachings of the Apostles and my own, and by his learning illustrated the Church. Those precious stones, and especially that magnificent one on his breast, which betokens the pure sentiments that animated him for the defence of the faith and to which he gave utterance in his works, are indicative of this. Those gems and especially the largest, symbolize the numerous books and other fruits of his mental labors. His glory is like unto mine, but he surpasses me by his crown of virginity."—

**) The black mantle worn by the Dominicans.
***) The white habit of the Dominicans.

The same witness testified that he had heard Brother Nicholas of Marsiliaco, Councillor and Chaplain to the King of Cyprus, and who had, at Paris, been the scholar of Brother Thomas of Aquin, say: "Brother Anthony, I was with Brother Thomas at Paris, and I tell thee before God that never have I seen one endowed with such purity as he."

In the attestation upon oath of the Abbot Thomas of Mathia, Canon of Salerno, it appears that he had at one time spoken in rather contemptuous terms of St. Thomas; but after having been miraculously reprimanded for the same and by a second miracle cured, he ever after felt great confidence in him. Once, when attacked by a temptation of the flesh, and about to commit a sin with full deliberation, he suddenly commended himself to Brother Thomas of Aquin, and the evil thoughts were entirely dissipated. From that time he more than once invoked the name of Brother Thomas, and always with similar results.—Try the same, dear friend. Invoke the saint often, yes, daily. Then wilt thou be sure of relating many victories.

CONSIDERATION FOR THE THIRD SUNDAY.

The Solid Humility of St. Thomas.

"*Humilitas facit hominem capacem Dei.*"
"Humility draws a man near to God."
(St. Thomas, Expos. in Matth. cp. XI.)

FIRST POINT.—Consider how St. Thomas of Aquin sought from youth to ground himself in humility. To be able to submit one's own will and to take a place below others, is a sign of genuine magnanimity; as, on the contrary, to look upon neglect or reproof as an injury, bespeaks narrow-mindedness. Great souls are great in this, that they clearly discern and acknowledge their own indigence and helplessness in many affairs; whilst the less-gifted deceive themselves as to their own ability. The great Master, St. Thomas, was endowed with a noble, an elevated soul, which easily understood the defects of the human mind, and upon which had been lavished the highest favors of God. But we must not fancy that humility was his by right. No; he had to win this virtue for himself, he had to strengthen, perfect, and preserve it. If the Breviary says of him on his feast: "O munus Dei gratiae, vincens quodvis miraculum, pestiferae superbiae nunquam persensit stimulum." O gift of God's grace, excelling every wonder: the poisonous sting of pride he never felt!".... Yet it was his constant care to guard the lowly virtue. What his biographers relate on this point of the time of his early studies, is both affecting and instructive.

The young novice was skilful in hiding his talents so that his fellow-students in the lecture-hall of the great Albert of Cologne, deceived by his constant silence and modest reserve, concluded that it was merely a cloak to conceal his real mental incapacity. They named him in consequence (which certainly bespoke little love on their part) "The Dumb Ox of Sicily." One of them more compassionate than the rest, offered to repeat with him the Master's discourse, that thereby he might more easily keep pace with his companions in study. Almighty God permitted that one day the kind-hearted Samaritan came to a difficult passage which he could not unravel. It was now Thomas's turn to explain the knotty question. This incident gave occasion to that famous saying of Blessed Albertus in which he predicted the future greatness of his silent scholar. In presence of the whole school, he called on young Thomas to solve the problem upon which his fellow-students had stranded. And when Thomas had done so in the most brilliant manner, Albertus gave utterance to the celebrated words: "We call this young man a dumb ox; but the bellowings of his doctrine will one day resound throughout the whole world." St. Thomas, silent as before retired quietly and humbly to his place; not that he ignored his mental gifts, but he ascribed the honor to Him alone who had so richly endowed him. *That is humility!* The consciousness that of ourselves we are nothing and have nothing; that all is from God, that all honor therefrom must flow back to God—that *is humility!* Therefore does St. Thomas say:—"Humility, in whatever way it is taken, lowers one." For since all good is from God, there can be no grounds for self-exaltation.

Now ask thyself what magnificent gifts are thine that thou shouldst so pride thyself upon them? In what qualification dost thou surpass St. Thomas? Should not that very question itself when applied to thee fill thee with humiliation? If thou art persuaded that all thy talents, thy excellent parts, thy skill, thy beauty, &c., are not from thyself and do not to thee belong, that God can withdraw them from thee in one moment—how, then, canst thou presume to boast? He that has nothing, that is nothing in his own eyes, that does not exalt himself, but willingly submits to others—he is truly humble. "Humility alone," says St. Augustine, "is the foundation of the spiritual edifice." —Hear how St. Thomas explains this: "The acquisition of the virtues is, as it were, the raising of a spiritual edifice, of which the first must be the foundation. For this acquisition a twofold operation is necessary: the removal of obstacles and the laying of the foundation by drawing near to God. The last is effected by faith; consequently, faith is, in a much higher sense than humilty, the foundation of the edifice. But humility is, also, the foundation in the first signification, since it removes the principal obstacle; viz., pride, which God must ever resist. Humility suppresses the swellings of pride, makes the soul submissive and thereby susceptible of the influx of divine grace. That is the meaning of the short saying of St. Thomas at the head of to-day's consideration: "Humility draws a man near to God."

How often will grace remain sterile, if the mind, involved in vain-glorious darkness and puffed up by the fumes of self-conceit, attributes to itself the successful results of its good works even before it is attained! Is not that, perhaps, the cause of the ill-success of the works of many men and the evident malediction that lies upon them? Dost thou wish to deprive thy life, thy actions, of energy and merit? All thou needest for that end is, to labor with pride and self-exaltation. Do this and thou mayest be sure that all will be radically spoiled. But wouldst thou attract a blessing upon all thou dost? Then give to God alone the honor. Each will then have what belongs to him: God the glory, and thou His blessing.

SECOND POINT.—Consider further that St. Thomas far from allowing his humility to be compromised by the great fame of his genius and learning, became as years rolled on only the more deeply rooted therein. The conviction of his own weakness and of God's unique title to everything like honor, had so firm a hold upon him that his humility was never endangered. The honor of Almighty God and the victory of the truth, were the only ends he had in view in all his writings and discourses. It is said of him that in child-like simplicity he once gave utterance to the following expressions: "I thank God that the thought of my learning, my pulpit orations, or my public disputations have never given rise to an emotion of vain-glory that could elevate my soul from the low place of humility. If, through surprise, such an emotion intruded itself, it was instantly suppressed by an act of the understanding."—Hence arose his contempt for posts of honor in this world. Pope Clement IV., who valued him most highly, offered him different ecclesiastical distinctions. But the humble Master firmly rejected them. And when the same Pontiff sent him the Bull nominating him Archbishop of Naples, he not only declined the honor, but implored the Holy Father never again to press upon him such posts. When, at last, on his journey to the Council of Lyons, whither the Holy Father, Gregory X., had summoned him, his companion, Brother Reginald thus addressed him: "Master, you are going to the Council from which much good will accrue to the whole Church, to our Order, and to the kingdom of Sicily,"—to which Thomas replied: "God grant it!"—Reginald continued: "You and Brother Bonaventure will be raised to the Cardinalate, and each of you will thereby reflect honor upon his Order."—After a few more remarks of the same kind, Thomas cut the conversation short with the words: "Rest assured that my position will never be other than it is at present."

That is practical humility. It consists not merely in beautiful words, but it shows itself upon occasions in which one might easily be entrapped. What thousands of others would have grasped with both hands, the solid humility of St. Thomas determined him to refuse, in order that he might continue in his vocation, that of a poor, simple religious. Whilst many pass their whole life in aiming at distinctions, one higher than the other; whilst they are vexed and chagrined when their elevation comes too slowly for their wishes, or when others outstrip them in the race; the truly humble man is never happier than when kept in a retired position, when no honors are offered him, when he has no distinction to refuse. Now ask thyself seriously and answer the question truthfully: How dost thou stand in the struggle with that high soaring and yet grovelling desire after honor? At what art thou aiming with so much striving and eagerness? The honor of God alone, or thine own aggrandizement?—Is it hard for thee to bear a rebuff, a reprimand upon occasions in which thou believest thyself deserving of better treatment? or from persons having no right to interfere in thy affairs? Is the portrait of the humble man as depicted by Blessed Albertus Magnus, the teacher of St. Thomas, applicable to thee?—"The truly humble man fears only that some honor might be shown him ; and if such a thing should happen to him, he is interiorly alarmed and distressed at it;.... he compares himself with no one, neither his superiors, his inferiors, nor yet with his equals, for he esteems himself the last of all. He despises no one but himself; he desires ardently to be despised by all the world, and sincerely rejoices in contempt. Such a man fears no dishonor, because he loves no honor."— O how must they be disposed, how must they live who can so openly, so energetically discuss the subject of humility, without fear of their actions giving the lie to their words! Shall I not try to reach this degree of humility and, like my holy protector, acquire the love of my own abjection? Not the position appointed me by Almighty God is incompatible with humility ; but the striving after something above what God's will has assigned me— that is incompatible with humility. To be the highest of the angels, was not for Lucifer a sin; but to wish to rise to the throne of God, was the cause of his fall into hell. The recognition of true merit and the glory consequent on the same, do not rob a man of humility; but to be in love with such recognition and such glory, would prove destructive of the virtue in question. No; I will be neither so bold nor so foolish as to usurp the rights of God. I will, in deepest humility, follow St. Thomas till death. I will imitate his self-abnegation, and beg him to assist me in my efforts.

Prayer.

O great St. Thomas, radiant, magnificent star of Holy Church, who wast at the same time so humble and modest, thou wast entirely free from the sting of that horrible and grievous vice which thou didst so clearly portray as the most frightful wandering, as the greatest estrangement from God, and the most deplorable of all sins! O how confused am I at the sight of thy greatness which knew so well how to humble itself! Yes, thou art the teacher of truth, for thou didst practise the truth thou didst proclaim in terms so touchingly beautiful! Humility is truth. Humility is the acknowledgment that we deserve degradation only, and that honor belongs to God alone. O help me, St. Thomas, not to comprehend something of this truth, for it is so clear that only the insanity of pride could fail to see it; but help me to practise it, since I cannot do that without great grace. Hardly does a humiliation menace me, when I begin to shrink from it; my pride rises up; reasons are multiplied against it; and I leave no means untried, how suspicious soever they may be, in order to avert the dreaded calamity. Ah, have pity on me! Fail not to assist me as often as my stupid pride gets the mastery and leads me to behave in a manner so unworthy of a scholar of Him who was God, but who at the same time said: "Learn of Me that I am meek and humble of heart."—Full of confidence in thy assistance, O humble and yet mighty protector, I will daily practise those virtues that, for the very reason of thy greatness, shine so conspicuously in thee, O thou man of giant intellect, thou infallible teacher of the Church, thou renowned oracle of our day! O great and humble St. Thomas, make me as humble as thyself!

Prayer of the Church.
(Page 17.)

Trait from the Life of St. Thomas of Aquin.

Of the astonishing humility of St. Thomas, his first biographer gives the following example: "On one of his journeys, the saint stopped at the monastery of his Order in Bologna. Whilst walking up and down one of the corridors absorbed in meditation, a Brother from another convent and who knew not the saint approached. Having the Prior's permission to take the first one he should happen to meet as a companion into the city, he addressed Thomas, saying. "Good Brother, the

Prior says that you must come with me."—The saint bowed his head and followed him. Not being able, on account of the painful state of his feet, to keep pace with the Brother, he more than once received a reproof for his lagging, in answer to which he humbly begged pardon. The townsfolk, to whom the great teacher was known and dear, saw with amazement and compassion the renowned Master slowly and painfully following a simple lay-brother. They guessed the true state of the case, and forgave the poor brother on account of his ignorance. But when they informed him who it was that he was dragging around in such a style, he was confounded, and begged Thomas's forgiveness, pleading his ignorance as an excuse. The townspeople made no secret of their astonishment. They questioned Thomas reverentially as to how he could humble himself so deeply? The holy Master answered: "The religious state consists in obedience, by which man subjects himself to man for God's sake, as God subjected Himself to man for man's sake."—Let us see how St. Thomas judged of his own writings, of which a Pope has said: "So many articles, so many miracles!"— Shortly before his death, he suddenly discontinued his work on his great Summa. At the oft-repeated questions and solicitations of his friend and companion, Brother Reginald of Piperno, the saint, at last exclaimed: "All that I have written appears to me as so much rubbish, compared with what I have seen, and what has been revealed to me!"

Such humility is a greater proof of sanctity than all miracles could be.

CONSIDERATION FOR THE FOURTH SUNDAY.

St. Thomas's Indefatigable Ardor in the Search after Sacred Wisdom.

> "*Haec doctrina maxime sapientia est inter omnes sapientias humanas, non quidem in aliquo genere tantum, sed simpliciter.*"
>
> "This science (Theology) is, of all human sciences the highest. It excels all others, not in this or that point only, but it is simply above them all."
>
> (Summa Theol. I. qu. I. a. 6.)

FIRST POINT.—Consider the exalted idea that St. Thomas had of divine wisdom. To it he applied the words of the Holy Ghost in the Book of Proverbs: "She hath sent her maids to invite to the tower," and he declared these maids to be all the other sciences in comparison with that which treats of God. He shows how the different sciences serve partly for the culture of the understanding, and partly for the practical affairs of life. But sacred science ranks above both; for the sciences that appertain to mental culture hold their rank either from the certainty to which they lead, or from the elevated subjects of which they treat. Whilst all human sciences derive their certainty from the imperfect light of reason alone, heavenly science is based upon the light of divine knowledge, which is subject neither to limit nor illusion. This divine doctrine comprehends things far transcending reason, whilst the rest of the sciences touch upon only what is within its reach. Of the practical sciences, the more excellent is that which has a higher aim in view; therefore does this holy science again transcend all others, inasmuch as it tends to the highest aim, eternal happiness.

Hence it is also the highest widom. Wisdom, in any art or branch of knowledge, regulates all minor rules of action in conformity with some one leading cause; but sacred science fixes its eye upon the highest cause of the universe, upon God Himself, and from this supreme standpoint, it determines all the rest. The esteem in which an object is held, is always the preliminary condition of love. We may conclude, therefore, from the high esteem St. Thomas entertained for sacred science, with what love and earnestness he devoted himself to it. Once, he was returning with some of his scholars from St. Denis near Paris, where they had venerated the holy relics and visited the monks. As they approached Paris from a point whence they could command a view of the whole city, one of his scholars said to Thomas: "Master, how beautiful is this city, this Paris!"—"Yes, very beautiful," was the reply. "Would that it belonged to you!"—continued the scholar. "What should I do with it?"—asked Thomas. The other answered: "You could sell it to the King of France and with the proceeds build monasteries for the Friars-Preachers." But Thomas closed the conversation with: "Indeed, I should far rather have the Homilies of St. Chrysostom upon the Gospel of St. Matthew; for if this city were mine, the care of its management would rob me of leisure for the consideration of heavenly things, and thus mar the peace of my soul."—In the process of canonization, a witness testified that he had heard the above from many, for that word of the holy Master became universally known at Paris. A single work upon God and His kingdom, was more valued by the great Master than the possession of a metropolis. He dreaded temporal goods that might put an obstacle to his study of the highest wisdom.

What is my fervor for the things of God? for the knowledge of the divine doctrine of our holy faith and of the Commandments whose observance is a condition for the gaining of eternal life? Is that not truly realized in me which St. Thomas only feared for himself—that earthly possessions and the care of temporal things, might disturb and hinder the flight of his soul into higher regions? Am I not of the number of those that hold all things dearer than the truths revealed by God? And yet these truths are the highest wisdom, since every other science must either subserve this, or become hurtful and absurd. It is, perhaps, my vocation, or at times my secret desire, to devote myself to the priesthood, to the religious life; and yet I do not find in my efforts after knowledge those high aspirations to which St. Thomas so significantly alludes when he calls sacred wisdom the mistress, and all other branches of knowledge her maids. And though I may not be called by God to instruct others, is not a certain degree of knowledge of holy religion necessary to every Christian, to all men, as a condition of love? Does not indifference to what is holy originate in ignorance? Does not the little esteem for religious truths arise from the deplorably superficial treatment they receive? Ought not the deep and solid comprehension of the doctrines and commandments of our holy religion together with the connection existing among them, excite in my breast real enthusiasm for them? In a word, does not my little appreciation of the treasure spring from my ignorance of its worth?

Ah, my holy Master, it must not continue thus! Thou hast taken the proper standpoint, and thou hast also shown it to me. If God is our highest aim, our true happiness, there can be nothing so worthy our serious consideration as the ways that lead to Him, or upon which He comes to meet us. After the example of St. Thomas, I will love and treasure above every thing else the sacred knowledge of God and His kingdom; and I will often recall those words of Jesus in His pontifical prayer before His Passion: "But this is eternal life, that they may know Thee, the only true God, and Jesus Christ whom Thou hast sent." (John XVII. 3.)

SECOND POINT.—Consider further upon what way the Angelic Master arrived at this highest wisdom, and how that way chosen by him helped him to attain that eminence which makes him the admiration of the whole Church. What our Holy Father, Leo XIII., expressed with so much conviction before the entire world, is only the echo of the universal judgment of Holy Church, a judgment held from the days of the saint down to our own. As Gregory X. hoped for the greatest results from St. Thomas's presence at the Council of Lyons; so at those of Florence and Trent, the *Summa* of the saint was laid by the Holy Scriptures in the midst of the assembled Fathers. Pope Innocent VI. says of the holy Doctor: "The Written Word of God excepted, I find in no teacher a greater keenness of expression, a more correct form of doctrine, more solid views, or a better manner of presenting the truth than in St. Thomas. He that follows his opinions, never errs; but whoever contradicts him, has at all times been looked upon with suspicion."

Whence had the great Master his knowledge? He himself declared to his friend and companion, Brother Reginald Piperno, that his learning proceeded not from natural gifts alone, but from the inspiration of the Holy Spirit; for never had he sat down to write without invoking with tears help from Heaven. If a doubt or difficult question arose, he returned to prayer, certain that an outpouring of his own heart would attract light upon the case in hand. With the exception of the little time devoted to sleep and the refection barely necessary to keep up his physical strength, his days and nights were given wholly to meditation, prayer, reading, preaching, writing, and dictating. Even during recreation with his brethren, his mind was so absorbed by his loved holy science that, at the close of the exercise, he could return to his books without distraction. When he found himself unable to solve some difficulties in the Prophet Isaias, he resorted to prayer and fasting, in which he continued until the solution was brought him from Heaven. One night the Princes of the Apostles, Sts. Peter and Paul, appeared to him; and after a long conversation, to which his friend Reginald listened attentively, the saintly Master dictated in rapid succession to his astonished amanuensis the difficulties and their solution, as if reading from a book. "O happy Master," exclaims his biographer when relating this fact," to whom Heaven's janitor unlocks the portals of Holy Scripture; to whom Paul, who marvellously scaled the heights celestial, unfolds the mysteries of truth!"

We boast and hear others boasting of the wonderful progress of our century. So be it! But whence comes it that its knowledge is unfruitful, unproductive of either solid results or spiritual consolation? Why is it that our clever men make less use of their intellectual acquirements in the attainment of true and lasting happiness than would an illiterate peasant? Whence is it that we ourselves with all our successful undertakings taste so little real satisfaction, are so little solicitous for the rescuing of the human race from eternal destruction? Ah, it is because our science is not from God, does not tend to God, is not employed for God! "He that soweth not with me," says Jesus, "scattereth."

Now, how is it with myself? Shall I not act wisely and discreetly by drawing waters from the highest sources? Only the blessing of Heaven confers success. When St. Thomas was appointed to take the degree of Doctor at the University of Paris, his humility was shocked, and he prayed earnestly. During the night, a venerable old man appeared to him, consoled him, and said: "Take no other words than these: 'Thou waterest the hills from Thy upper rooms: the earth shall be filled with the fruit of Thy work.'" That was truly the text most suitable to the great Doctor, for in it lies the prophecy of his success throughout all ages. I will bear in mind the most significant of those words: "From Thy upper rooms." If every good gift comes from above, from the Father of Light, it must be especially true of that heavenly wisdom which enlightens us upon God and our relations to Him. Gladly will I adopt the views and practice of the holy Master, who declares that books are only the external help, and study only the human condition for acquiring true wisdom; but that enlightenment from on high can alone infuse spirit into the dead letter, can alone render true wisdom attainable. Prayer and unremitting application must go hand in hand, that I may penetrate deeper and deeper into those mysteries that alone are deserving the efforts of an immortal spirit. My eternity will then be the perfecting of what I have begun upon earth: to know God and love Him above all things.

Prayer.

"God of my fathers, and Lord of mercy, who hast made all things with Thy word, and by Thy wisdom hast appointed man, that he should have dominion over the creature that was made by Thee, give me wisdom that sitteth by Thy throne, and cast me not off from among Thy children: for I am Thy servant and the Son of Thy handmaid, a weak man, and of short time and falling short of the understanding of judgment and laws. Send her out of Thy holy heaven and from the throne of Thy majesty, that she may be with me and labor with me, that I may know what is acceptable with Thee; for by wisdom they were healed, whosoever have pleased Thee, O Lord, from the beginning." (Wisdom IX. 1, 2, 4, 5, 10, 19).

Thou didst, O Lord, fill Thy servant, St. Thomas, with incomparable, heavenly wisdom, so that in very truth, can the whole Church satiate her hunger with the fruits of his works! Give me a little spark of his illumination signified by the sun upon his breast. Give me a ray of his celestial light that by it my path through life may be lit up and that, if it be Thy holy will, I may enkindle it in others.

Pray for me, O great and wonderful Master, that I may imitate Thee in this wherein all may follow Thy example, that I may keep my eyes always turned heavenward. As the eagle seizes its young and bears it on high, in order to sharpen its gaze by fixing it upon the sun; so do thou raise me up, that my eyes may now become accustomed to look upon the Sun of eternal brightness and thence to draw eternal happiness. Obtain for me, St. Thomas, what the Church bids me ask on Thy feast: viz., to understand what thou didst teach, and in my life to follow what thou didst practise. Through Christ, our Lord. Amen.

Prayer of the Church.
(Page 17.)

Trait from the Life of St. Thomas of Aquin.

In the process of canonization an eye-witness attested that St. Thomas had risen entirely from the earthly to the divine. He used to become so absorbed in lofty thoughts at table that the viands before him might be removed without his remarking it. The following instance of this is recorded: St. Thomas was once invited to the table of St. Louis, King of France, but he excused himself as he was at that time engaged upon his great *Summa*. The king however, would take no refusal. He obtained from the Prior of the monastry at Paris a command for the holy Master to dine at the royal table. St. Thomas went immediately on the word of his superior, but full of thoughts that had occupied him in his cell. As he was sitting by the king's side, suddenly a truth flashed upon his mind like a streak of lightning—and he struck the table with his hand exclaimiug: "Now is the heresy of the Manicheans at an end!"—The Prior, who sat next to him greatly embarrassed, said: "Master Thomas, remember, you are at the table of the King of France!"—and then he seized the saint's mantle, and shook him till he came to himself. Thomas, understanding what had happened, bowed toward the holy king and begged pardon for having been so absent-minded in his presence. St. Louis was filled with admiration, and thought only of recording the lights that the holy Doctor had drawn from divine inspiration. He sent for his secretary to take down at the saint's dictation what the Spirit of God had imparted to him.—It was a similar love of wisdom that raised both these saints to similar honors in the Church of God. Do thou, also, esteem the teaching of St. Thomas, and thou, too, wilt become holy.

CONSIDERATION FOR THE FIFTH SUNDAY.

St. Thomas and the Most Blessed Sacrament.

"*Tantum ergo Sacramentum, Veneremur cernui.*"
"Down in adoration falling,
Lo! the Sacred Host we hail."
(Hymn "*Pange Lingua.*" St. Thomas.)

FIRST POINT.—Consider the first words quoted above taken from St. Thomas's "Pange Lingua" —"Tantum ergo Sacramentum," "*The great Sacrament.*"—No doctor has ever spoken or written in language so clear, so precise, or so beautiful of that holiest mystery of Jesus Christ's love as St. Thomas has done. No one has ever shown forth the magnificent greatness of that astonishing miracle as he has done. No one has ever succeeded as he in treating of the Most Blessed Sacrament of our Holy Church in expressions so exact, so intelligible, and so circumstantial. His words are like sunbeams revealing to the mind the truth that most of all redounds to the honor of that highest of all gifts; viz., that It is in very deed the "Tantum Sacramentum," the "Great Sacrament," so great as to be beyond the reach of human intellect or human praise. St. Thomas is the Doctor of the Most Blessed Sacrament. With what accuracy and keenness of expression, with what reverence and dignity of speech does he discourse on the wonderful mystery of the Body and Blood of Jesus Christ! He cooperated with Pope Urban IV., in 1264, in the institution of the feast of Corpus Christi, and was commissioned by the same Pontiff to compose the Mass and Office for the solemnity. He acquitted himself in such a manner as to lead us to believe that "he had thrown into human words an angel's song."—J. B. Canteuil, a celebrated writer of sacred canticles of the sixteenth century, uttered no exaggeration when he openly declared that he would give all his productions for the following strophe of one of St. Thomas's hymns:—

> *Se nascens dedit socium,*
> *Convescens in edulium,*
> *Se moriens in pretium,*
> *Se regnans dat in praemium.*
>
> "At birth, our brother He became;
> At board, Himself as food He gives;
> To ransom us He died in shame;
> As our reward, in bliss He lives."*

The eighty-four articles of the *Summa* which treat of the Most Blessed Sacrament, are the most

---

* Caswell's *Lyra Catholica*. (American Edition, p. 160.)

thorough of anything that has ever been written upon It in so narrow a space. Its title; the need men have of It Its matter and Its transubstantiation; the manner of Jesus' presence in It; the words of holy consecration; the effects of the Most Holy Mystery; the receiver and the dispenser, together with the ceremonies made use of at the Holy Sacrifice,—all are considered, and that with a dignity and calm security, as if the great Doctor held the Holy of Holies in his hands, as if every word were an act of reverential adoration. How sublime the whole signification, the grandeur, the power, the beneficent workings of the Holy Eucharist, as summed up by St. Thomas in the simple Antiphon: "*O sacrum convivium!*" —O sacred banquet, wherein Christ is received; the memorial of His Passion is celebrated; the mind is filled with grace; and a pledge of future glory is given unto us!"

The holy Master had even as a child sought God alone, had been intent upon God alone; consequently, he found Him everywhere, and treated Him as worthily as a weak creature could treat his God. It would, indeed, have been a miracle if he had not found God, especially in that Mystery of Love, in which Jesus abides in order to be "Our God with us."

Is this great Sacrament the sun around which thy life revolves? Are thy thoughts often turned toward Him who thinks of thee by day and night? His joy is to be with the children of men—is it the special privilege of thy life to tarry in His presence?

Holy Mother Church, in the jubilation of her heart, finds the highest expression of her rejoicing in the sacred songs of St. Thomas; and annually on the recurrence of the feast of Corpus Christi does she enkindle by them the fire of holy enthusiasm in the breast of her children, for it was partly to his efforts that the feast owes its origin.

Art thou, also, intent upon grasping the teachings of Holy Church upon the Adorable Eucharist, that thou mayest honor It, not through custom, but from the deep conviction that God Himself is hidden therein? *Tantum ergo, Sacramentum.* Hast thou treated God as God during the Holy Mass? when in the church? when passing the tabernacle? Art thou reverent during Holy Communion, maintaining a respectful silence is His presence, as the Holy Scripture enjoins: "The Lord is in His temple. Let the whole earth be silent before Him." In thy preparation for Holy Communion, dost thou reflect that God is coming to thee, God, whose sanctity can brook no sin? In thy thanksgiving, hast thou not treated the "Great Sacrament" slightingly? And when at a distance, far from the church, do thy thoughts go back to thy God in the tabernacle before which burns the perpetual light, to remind thee of His uninterrupted presence there and to stand before Him as a symbol of thine own true love for Him?

O Jesus, Holy Host, wonderful Sacrament! up to the present much of all this has been wanting to me! To facilitate my access to Thee, Thou didst become little, Thou didst conceal Thy majesty; therefore did I, in my wretchedness, forget that Thou art the great God, my Judge! I hear sung, "Tantum ergo Sacramentum "—"The Great Sacrament," and my ears have grown accustomed to their sound. I sing, I repeat listlessly those words that should act as reminders. But it shall be so no more! I will choose St. Thomas as my special patron in all that concerns the Most Holy Eucharist; for he who excelled all others in so many particulars, has even excelled himself in his praise, his reverence, and his love toward the Holy Mystery.

SECOND POINT.—Consider St. Thomas in his love and devotion to the Holy Sacrifice of the Mass. He is not only the Doctor, he is also the adorer of this great miracle: "*Tantum ergo Sacramentum, Veneremur cernui.*"—His conviction of the greatness of this divine Gift was not sterile; it was deep, living, and effective.

Daily, when not prevented by illness, he celebrated the Holy Mass, and assisted at a second, at which he frequently served. Often during the Holy Sacrifice, his devotion glowed with such fervor as to draw from him streams of tears. Once on Passion Sunday whilst devoutly celebrating in the monastery of his Order at Naples, he became enraptured in presence of many of the nobility and, for a long time, remained motionless, until his astonished brethren, by gently pushing and touching him, recalled him from his deep contemplation. His devotion at the Holy Sacrifice was attested on oath by many of the witnesses at the process of his canonization. Some affirmed that, on the days upon which he could not himself celebrate, he assisted at two Masses. It was during the Holy Sacrifice that his approaching death was revealed to him. In all his doubts, he went to the altar and there remained in tearful prayer until light came to him. When on his death-bed, he requested the most holy Viaticum as his end drew near. When the Abbot of the Cistercian monastery of Fossa Nova, where Thomas lay ill on his journey to the Council of Lyons, brought him the Blessed Sacrament, he arose in spite of his weakness and hastened in tears to meet his Lord. He threw himself on his knees, saluted Him, and prayed in words that inspired the listeners with wonder. To the customary question as to whether he believed present in the Host the true Son of God, born of the Virgin Mary, and who for us had suffered, he answered with tears: "If in this life there were given greater certainty upon the Blessed Sacrament than that which the faith affords, yet would I answer with the latter that I believe as true and hold as certain this to be the true God and Man, Son of the Eternal Father and the Virgin Mary. And so I believe in heart and confess in words, as has just been said by the priest of this Most Holy Sacrament."—Then before receiving he exclaimed: "I receive Thee, the price of my soul's redemption, for love of whom I have studied, I have watched, and I have labored! Thee have I preached, Thee have I taught! Against Thee never have I breathed a word, neither am I wedded to my own opinion. If I have held aught that is untrue regarding this Blessed Sacrament, I subject it to the judgment of the Holy Roman Church, in whose obedience I now pass out of life."

Doubtless, thou, too, wouldst wish to speak thus beautifully of the Blessed Sacrament at the close of thy career upon earth.—And that thou canst do if, during thy life, thy love for It has been like unto that of St. Thomas. Think not that thine eye will be able to gaze into eternal light, if thou dost not exercise it now behind the veil that conceals the Divinity; or that thy heart can be warm in death, if in life thou hast stood afar from the furnace. The general laws of nature repeat themselves in the sphere of the spirit, corresponding however still more perfectly and with greater security to the province in which they work. As the forces of nature cannot influence one another without some degree of proximity; so must nearness to God increase love for Him, and removal from Him weaken the same, the effect produced being greater or less in proportion to our ardor in His service. The nearer the iron approaches the magnet, the more powerful is the influence of the latter upon it. Could it be possible that I should draw near to the Magnet of hearts, should often be found in Its presence, without experiencing Its powerful effects?—Ah, the future must find me quite changed with regard to the Holy Eucharist! The words of St. Thomas on his deathbed have brought light to my soul: "I receive Thee, Thou Consoler of my pilgrimage, Thou for whom I have studied, labored, watched, preached, and taught."-I receive Thee before whom my whole life should be one uninterrupted adoration, one everlasting "Tantum ergo Sacramentum, Veneremur cernui."—Jesus in the Blessed Sacrament should be the desire of our heart, the motive power of all our actions, the centre around which should circle all our aspirations and longings, the beneficent sun of our labor by day, the gently beaming moon of our rest or dangers by night. Jesus in the Divine Eucharist should ever be our dearest Friend, to Him should we take joy and sorrow, from Him seek strength and courage, at His feet lay gain and honor, in Him alone find all our happiness. The lamp before His tabernacle should be the brightest and dearest star in life, that He whom it symbolizes may fill us with what Holy Mother Church will ask for each one of us after death: "And may perpetual light shine upon him!"

Prayer.

O glorious bard of the Most Blessed Mystery of our altars, St. Thomas! How shall I praise thee and love thee as thou deservest for having placed before us, in all Its majesty and beauty, the great Mystery of the love of Jesus Christ, for having shown us in thine own life how to venerate that Miracle of God's power! Thou thyself dost serve us as a model in this. From the glowing treasures of thine own heart, thou dost place upon our lips the words most fitting and most beautiful, with which we are to praise, to magnify, to adore, and to love this highest and holiest of all the Sacraments. Thy thoughts, thy words, thy labors, thy whole life, form one continuous "Pange Lingua," one unbroken "Adoro Te." Thou hast enabled us in those heavenly sounds to do homage to our God upon earth, to hail Him in songs of joy. They truly express the praises of the angelic throng, since they come to us from thy lips, O thou angel upon earth! O help me, Angelic Master, that the Bread of Angels, of which thou singest:

> "Lo! upon the altar lies,
> Hidden deep from human eyes,
> Bread of angels from the skies,
>   Made the food of mortal man;
> Children's meat to dogs denied" ....

may be in very deed to me the "Children's Bread!" Stand by me, teach me, and obtain for me the divine assistance, that I may not draw upon myself a refusal when I sing before the Most Blessed Sacrament thy words: "Sic nos tu visita, sicut te colimus," "Do Thou visit us, even as we honor Thee."—With heart and lips will I repeat the words, seeking day by day to understand them better, which Holy Church from thee learned and has already rehearsed innumerable times: O God, who hast left us in this wonderful Sacrament a perpetual memorial of Thy Passion: grant us, we beseech Thee, so to reverence the sacred mysteries of Thy Body and Blood, that we may continually find in our soul the fruit of Thy Redemption: Thou who livest and reignest, world without end. Amen.

Prayer of the Church.
(Page 17.)

Trait from the Life of St. Thomas of Aquin.

The Angelic Doctor was about thirty-two years years old when there arose in the University of Paris a dispute among the Doctors and Professors, upon the manner of Jesus' presence in the Holy Eucharist. After long arguments for and against, they agreed to leave the solution of the debated question to the young Thomas whose mental ascendancy was already felt and acknowledged. The opinion of the several Doctors was handed him in writing and his decision awaited. Thomas, according to custom, became lost in contemplation, prayed ardently, and then exposed his own convictions on the question in words short, but strictly conclusive. But he would not submit the result of his labor to the University without high approbation. He approached the altar, laid thereon his manuscripts, raised his eyes to the Lord, and prayed: "Lord Jesus Christ, Thou who art truly present in this wonderful Sacrament and who dost operate that which I am to declare, I implore Thee if what, with Thy help, I have written about Thee, is true, permit me to teach it openly but if I have written anything contrary to faith and not in conformity with its teachings upon Thy holy Sacraments, let it be condemned."

Then his confreres, who were closely watching him, saw Christ suddenly appear over the writing that Thomas had laid on the altar, and heard the words: "Well hast thou written, Thomas, concerning this Sacrament of My Body; and well hast thou solved the problem—that is to say, in as far as it is possible for one to do so who still is prisoner in the flesh."—At the same time the observers beheld the holy Doctor hovering in the air, a whole yard above the floor. He remained so long in this position, that they had time to call the Prior of the monastery and many of the Brothers to witness the astonishing spectacle. After that divine approval, the holy Doctor went to the University where he spoke so fluently and lucidly upon the disputed point that all embraced his opinion. And well they might, since He whom it most nearly concerned had, first of all, given His approbation!

CONSIDERATION FOR THE SIXTH SUNDAY.

St. Thomas's Love for Mary.

*"Felix doctor, cujus solatio
Angelorum servit attentio;
Petrus, Paulus favent obsequio,
Dei mater mulcet alloquio."*

"O blessed Doctor, thou whom the angels served, to whom Peter and Paul brought light in doubt, and whom the Mother of God sweetly comforted!"
(Dominican Breviary for the Feast of St. Thomas.)

FIRST POINT.—Consider the love of the Angelic Doctor for Mary. His biographers find signs of it even in his childhood. (See Trait, end of the present consideration.) It is not at all to be wondered at that the Queen of Angels should have taken possession of the Angel of the Schools even in his earliest days. The greatest minds have always been powerfully attracted to Mary, who is justly saluted as the Seat of Wisdom. As Jesus gathered around Him virginal souls; viz., Mary, Joseph, John, so too does Mary draw after her the innocent, the virginal, the pure. It would have been strange, indeed, if St. Thomas who, as we know, always carried about him a relic of St. Agnes, such was his admiration for the spotlessness of the saint, had not most tenderly loved and devoutly honored the Immaculate Virgin of virgins.

The holy Doctor has given us sufficient points in his own life and writings, to indicate clearly his love for the Queen of Heaven. In this he imitates St. Bernard, that ardent lover of the Mother of God; and the fact of his having given up his soul to God in a Cistercian monastery which, like almost all the churches of this Order, was dedicated to the Blessed Virgin, was certainly not due to what we call chance. The great Angel of the Schools maintained what at that time in the Church was the clearly and openly expressed opinion, and spoke of Mary as only the most zealous servant of the glorious Virgin could speak. He taught of her in his explanation of the Angelical Salutation: "She is called full of grace," because she had in her soul the fulness of grace, no sins but all virtues. From her soul the blessings of grace flowed out upon her body and prepared her to be the dwelling-place of the Son of God. Yes, even upon all mankind, upon all their needs and dangers flow streams from her plenitude of grace. Help and strength are given by her to every virtue, for to her is applied this verse of the Canticles: "A thousand bucklers" hang upon this tower of David against all the snares of the enemy; and this word of Ecclesiasticus finds in her its fulfilment: "In me is all hope of life and of virtue."— She far excels the angels, as well in grace and riches as in nearness to God; for to the angels, God stands in the relation of Lord, but to Mary in that of Son. Yes, she is higher than the angels themselves in purity; for she is not only pure in herself, but she helps others on to purity. No guilt, no malediction of sin ever weighed upon her. She brought forth without labor, lived without the pressure of a sense of guilt, and died without decay; for Mary's body and soul are in heaven.

Esteem is the foundation and preliminary condition of love. How great must the love of St. Thomas have been for Mary of whom he draws such a picture for himself and for the whole Church, of whom he is so fond of speaking! A secular witness in the Process of Canonization, John Blasius, a Neapolitan judge, and courtier of the Queen of Sicily, relates that he once heard St. Thomas preach a whole Lent upon the words: "Hail, Mary, full of grace, the Lord is with thee," and noticed that whilst speaking he kept his eyes shut, or raised in contemplation to heaven.

Truly would it be a privilege to hear an angel in human form discourse upon the grandeur of Mary, upon the mysteries that were wrought by her co-operation. That would, indeed, be an impressive sermon.

But dost thou not hear St. Thomas preach when thou sayest the holy Rosary? Is it not a greater privilege to be allowed to speak so familiarly, so confidently, like a little child, to Mary whom St. Thomas so magnified, whom he so dearly loved, than even to hear him sound her praises?—Hast thou hitherto rightly estimated this happiness? Hast thou ever reflected upon the honor thou enjoyest of being able to commune lovingly and heart to heart with the Queen of heaven as often as thou desirest? Such a privilege as this thou canst not enjoy with thy equals. Hast thou ever considered that it is a bad sign not to be on terms of intimacy with her without whom no grace can be received, since all graces flow through her hands? Dost thou understand that sermon of St. Thomas wherein he explains how Mary is full of grace? If she has the fulness of grace, it cannot be thought that any one can obtain a share in those treasures, excepting through the intercession of her to whom they are all intrusted.

Imitate thy Master, and make the firm resolution to place in Mary's hands thy salvation and the care of all things belonging to it. Resolve to remain sincerely devoted to her, and often to salute her with that "Ave" which an angel brought from heaven; upon which the Angel of the Schools so loved to discourse that, for a whole Lent, he found in it abundant matter for his sermons; and which he still oftener, yes, times innumerable, pronounced in prayer. Hail Mary! Hail Mary! Ah, he that loves the angel's "Ave," will himself become angelic! The Angelic Doctor is a living, speaking proof of this. In a manuscript of his renowned work, "Summa contra Gentiles," written in St. Thomas's own hand, the margins of every page bear the words: "Ave, Ave, Ave Maria!"

SECOND POINT.—Consider how Mary returns and rewards the love borne her. William of Thoco, one of St. Thomas's biographers, tells us that the holy Doctor, when on his death-bed, revealed to his friend and companion, Reginald of Piperno, for the honor of God and the consolation of his confrere, that the Blessed Virgin and glorious Mother of God had appeared to him and set his mind at rest with regard to his life and his learning. Whatever he earnestly begged of God through her, especially that he might never be forced to abandon the position of a simple religious, he had always obtained. "The holy Doctor," continued the narrator, "as all his confessors unhesitatingly declare, preserved his virginal purity; he was white as snow in soul and in body. The most powerful of women, the sweet Mother, does not confine herself to the choirs of the heavenly court; she deigns likewise to impart to the pilgrims of earth the consolation of her presence. Whilst reigning as queen near the throne of her Son, she casts her merciful eyes upon her poor children of earth. With good reason is it thought that she obtained for her devoted Doctor that learning which made him so famous, as well as the lily of chastity which he sacrificed to God and ever preserved inviolable.

Behold, my soul, the condition necessary for obtaining Mary's protection, *a pure heart!*—and this condition is one that she herself can bestow upon her clients, one that she can protect for them. Mary desires it and she, too, can obtain it; and not only that, but all good things and a thousand joys besides. To her is applied what is read in the Epistle on the feast of St. Thomas. It is indeed, said first of all of Divine Wisdom, but may likewise be referred to Mary, the Mother and the Seat of Eternal Wisdom: "Now all good things came to me together with her, and innumerable riches through her hands."

Certainly, thou art desirous of the blessing which through Mary is to be won. Without hesitation, wilt thou answer that thou wouldst be well pleased if she procured for thee the assurance of thy salvation and all other blessings attached thereto, such as St. Thomas received from the hand and lips of the most pure Virgin. It is in thy power to secure the maternal protection of the Queen of Heaven, of the Mother of God. "I love them that love me," so run the words of Holy Writ, and they are applied by the Church to the

Blessed Virgin, as also these others: "And they that in the morning early watch for me, shall find me."—Art thou still in the early morning of thy life?—O preserve thy innocence, that delicate blossom, thy first love for the Bride of the Holy Ghost! She will never permit that flower to wither and die. No; she will guard it against frost and cold; protect it from hail and thunderstorms; will provide for it dew, and rain, and warm sunshine; until the fruit unfolds from the blossom and gradually matures; until the first love shall have ripened into eternal love; and from a childish, half unconscious, tender, feeble affection, shall have changed into fidelity, valiant, pure, enduring, and firm as a rock. Fidelity to Mary is, at the same time, fidelity to her Divine Son Jesus and fidelity to God. But how often have I proposed all this to myself, and yet have not abided by it! Yes, all the resolutions that I have made during these six Sundays, the lights that I have received in the meditations upon my saintly teacher, the graces that he has obtained for me,—will they have any value, any consequences for eternity?—With joy can I say: Yes, consequences truly great and precious, if I obtain the protection of her to whom St. Thomas owes his lily of purity, as well as his wisdom. She formed of him an angel of purity and of wisdom. "Whoever calls Thomas an angel," exclaims one of his admirers," has praised him enough. Nothing more is left for him to say, and anything less would be too little. Yes, is not he an angel, who lives as chastely in the flesh as if he were without a body? And could he not be chaste who had imbibed the *Ave Maria* with his mother's milk!"

O how happy am I to have discovered this way to wisdom and holiness, to purity and knowledge! St. Thomas has trodden it, in order to show me how one can go to heaven by a path of roses; can join the choirs of angels; yes, can even become like to the angels. How sweet to stay near Mary and with her to labor! She is the dwelling-place of virtues, a medicine of life, an abyss of grace. All that is not God is less than Mary. God Himself could not have created a greater Mother than the Mother of God—and that great Mother, as soon as I wish it, will become my Mother, and will remain such as long as I allow her. She who bore in her arms Him who sustains the world, will help me to carry every sorrow. She is the throne of mercy, to which all may have access. No client of Mary will ever be lost. But he that does not piously honor her, is not her client; and he that does not love her, does not truly honor her; and no one that does not imitate her, loves her sincerely. I will, therefore, in future prove my love to Mary, and daily beg St. Thomas to help me to be faithful to her.

Prayer.

O Mary, glorious Mother of Jesus Christ, most pure Virgin, powerful Queen of heaven! Behold I come to thee sorrowful for my past infidelity. As to St. Thomas, so also to me hast thou given rich graces and blessings, yes, long before I could begin to salute thee; and thou didst not cease to love me long after I had grown tepid and negligent in thy service. O do not now abandon me, since my saintly Master has opened my eyes to see again how happy thy children are under thy protecting mantle and near thy pure heart! Now will I remain unshaken in my fidelity to thee, untiring in my efforts to bring others to thee; now will I constantly aim at procuring thee and thy children honor. Forsake me not, O Mother of Mercy! Thou art the Mother and special Patroness of the Order whose brighest ornament St. Thomas, under thy maternal assistance, became. Behold, I too will become a spiritual child of this holy family, whose chief duty it is to preach Jesus Crucified and, by their glowing words, to enkindle in the hearts of the faithful ardent love for thee, His Mother. As far as I can, I will engrave in all hearts, but first of all in my own, thy name in ineffaceable characters.

And do thou, O holy, angelic Master, thou the scholar, the lover, the preacher, the sacred Doctor of Mary, do thou teach me to love Mary with that pure, intelligent, faithful and persevering love with which thou, from thy early childhood until thy last hour, didst love her and of which thou didst give her daily and tender proofs! Ah, then, when I go into "the house of my eternity," I shall, in ecstacy of soul and jubilation of heart, pronounce that "Ave Maria," that sweet salutation, which produced so great an impression upon thee before thy infant tongue could lisp its accents!

Prayer of the Church. (Page 17.)

Trait from the Childhood of St. Thomas of Aquin.

St. Thomas's mother once went with some other ladies to the baths at Naples, followed by the nurse carrying the gifted child in her arms. The nurse set the little boy down in the bath-room, when he caught up (whence it came, we know not) a scrap of paper in his baby hand. Providence permitted it to fall in his way, in order to show forth in the child what he would become when grown to man's estate. The nurse, wishing to undress the little boy for his bath, tried in vain to open the tiny hand that held the paper. The child began to cry so piteously that the nurse desisted from her efforts, and left him in possession of his treasure. The bath over and the child reclothed, he was taken to his mother, his little hand still grasping the paper. The mother, heedless of his cries, forced open the hand, and found upon the paper it so tightly held nothing but the Salutation of the glorious Virgin: "Ave Maria."— Scarcely had she given it back to the child when he carried it hastily to his little mouth and swallowed it.—"It would seem," says his early biographer, "that he proclaimed as a child the saving doctrines he was to announce as a saint; for that scrap of paper containing the first words that heralded our salvation, did not fall in his way without the overshadowing guidance of the Holy Ghost."—And another cries out in astonishment: "The first nourishment of Thomas's childhood was the name of Mary! His tongue had tasted Mary before it began to praise her; he knew of Mary before he had heard of her; he was Mary's scholar long before he became the Angelic Doctor. He would not have written well of the Son, had he not spoken well of the Mother. Lend an ear to him when he speaks of Mary, for her Son from the cross testified that he had written well of Him. The cross of the dying Saviour was the pulpit of the Teacher, and from it fell the words that created Thomas a Doctor of the Church: 'Thou hast written well of Me.'"

THE ANGELIC MILITIA;

OR

The Confraternity of the Cord of St. Thomas of Aquin.

That glorious victory gained by St. Thomas in favor of virginal purity, is well known. It was to it that he first owed the title of "Angel." Later on the same was again accorded him, on account of his angelic wisdom. (See Consideration for the Second Sunday, p. 19.)

After that victory, two angels appeared and girded him with a celestial cord, saying: "Behold, we gird thee by the command of God with the girdle of chastity, which henceforth will never be imperilled. What human strength cannot obtain, is now bestowed upon thee as a celestial gift."— Thomas wore that girdle till the end of his life, at which time he discovered to his friend, Reginald of Piperno, the grace he had received. The heavenly girdle was presented to the ancient monastery of Vercelli in Piedmont, St. Thomas's mother-house, by John of Vercelli, who entered upon the office of General of the Order, in 1274, the year of the saint's death. There the sacred relic remained, even in spite of the efforts of the holy Pontiff, Pius V., to place it among the treasures of the Eternal City, until the suppression of the monastery under Napoleon I. The Prior of Vercelli, at that time, took it with him, intending to bestow it upon the first monastery that would be restored in the province. He did so when at Chieri near Turin, a house of the Order was re-opened, and since that time St. Thomas's girdle has continued in its possession.

It is formed of many fine threads, but of what material the sharpest eye is unable to decide. One end has a double loop through which the cord is drawn in girding. The part that goes around the waist, is flat, somewhat wider than a flattened straw; the other part consists of two fine, four-cornered cords, which are tied into fifteen knots all alike and of peculiar make. The whole length of the girdle is not quite one and a half metres.* The color, originally white is, through age and the repeated touching of other girdles, somewhat brown, or rather pearl-color.

About the year 1580, Father Cyprian Uberti, Inquisitor of that vicinity, in his love for St. Thomas and his zeal for holy purity, began to make girdles similar to the holy relic, to which they were touched and then distributed as a safeguard of chastity. He may have been incited thereto by the miraculous girding of the saintly Columba of Trochazano, of the Third Order of St. Dominic. She had come off victorious from a great danger that threatened her chastity. In a fierce temptation against holy purity, which she had taken upon herself to free another, she invoked St. Thomas, and was favored by an apparition of the saint who caused her to be girded by two angels.

---

* A metre = 39.37 in.

Under date of March 13, 1644, the Rector of the Jesuit college at Vercelli wrote, as follows: "Whole volumes could be filled with the favors that have flowed from the girdle of St. Thomas; and I know of graces bestowed upon persons of all ages and both sexes that could be attributed to his intercession alone."

Father Aurelius Corbellini of the Order of the Hermits of St. Augustine, testifies to similar favors. He says that he had induced a woman, who for years had led a dissolute life, and whom no admonitions could move, to wear the girdle of St. Thomas. In a few days she, who had been a public sinner, was changed to a model of continency. "That," writes the narrator, "we have seen with our own eyes, heard with our own ears. It was an evident fact, to which we set our own seal in the Name of the Lord."

Occurrences similar to the above prompted a Belgian Dominican, Father Francis Deurwerders to realize his idea of uniting all that wore these girdles of St. Thomas into a Confraternity under the title "Militia Angelica," or "Angelic Militia." With the concurrence of the Very Rev. Father-General of the Order, Vincent Candidus, he drew up the statutes and submitted them to the Faculty of Theology in Louvain for examination, in the year 1640. The Faculty interested themselves in the case, appointed their Dean protector of the Angelic Militia, and decreed that the day of the translation of St. Thomas's relics, the 28th of January, should be yearly celebrated as the principal feast of the

Confraternity. In 1659, the Angelic Militia was already introduced into the churches of the Dominican Order at Vienna, soon after at Palermo, Reggio, Naples, Venice, Ghent, Valencia, Saragossa, Modena, Florence, Toulouse, Barcelona, &c. Kings and queens soon girded themselves with this new safeguard of chastity; and especially did numbers of students of the universities wear the girdle of St. Thomas. In 1677, the chapter-general of the order resolved to petition the Holy See for an extension to the whole Order of the Indulgences which had already been granted to the Angelic Militia of some places. Pope Benedict XIII., himself a Dominican, granted the petition under date of May 26, 1727.

The greatest grace attached to the Confraternity is, indeed, the protection of the Angelic Doctor over purity of soul and body. By the permission of the General of the Order, John of Marinis, the members of the Angelic Militia have, since February 28, 1651, shared in all the holy Masses, prayers, vigils, fastings, penances, merits and good works of the whole Dominican Order in its three branches, as well in life as after death. This spiritual community of goods is sanctioned by the Holy See.

INDULGENCES

OF THE

Angelic Militia or Confraternity of the Cord of St. Thomas of Aquin.

Pope Innocent X., Sixtus V., Benedict XIII., Pius VII., Gregory XVI., and Leo XIII. have granted the following Indulgences to the Confraternity:—

I. Plenary Indulgences.

1. On the day of reception. (Conditions: worthy confession and Communion.)

2. On January 28th, the feast of the Translation of the Relics of St. Thomas, the chief feast of the Confraternity. (Conditions: Confession, Communion, Visit to the church of the Confraternity, and prayer in same for the intentions of the Holy Father.)

3. On the 7th of March, the feast of St. Thomas of Aquin. (Conditions as in No. 2, excepting in case some obstacle prevents a visit to the church of the Confraternity, a visit to the parish church may be substituted.)

(The Plenary Indulgence on the feast of St. Thomas is applicable to the poor souls in purgatory.)

4. On one day at option of every month, provided the prayer of St. Thomas for the preservation of chastity, (see p. 91, "My dear Jesus," &c.) has been daily recited, and on the day chosen the Sacraments are received, and in *any* church the usual prayers for gaining Indulgence are said.

5. The same Indulgence is granted once in the month for daily reciting the prayer "Chosen lily," &c. (Page 77.)

6. At the hour of death, after a contrite confession and Communion ; or, if that is not possible, if with contrition the holy name of Jesus is invoked vocally or mentally.

II. *Partial Indulgences.*

1. Seven years and seven quarantines for those members who, after receiving the Sacraments, visit a church of the Confraternity on the following days :

Christmas, Easter, Pentecost, Conversion of St. Paul (Jan. 25th); St. Gregory the Great (March 12th); St. Ambrose (April 4th); St. Vincent Ferrer (April 5th); St. Peter Martyr (April 29th); St. Mary Magdalen (July 22d); St. Dominic (Aug. 4th); the Assumption of Our Lady (Aug. 15th) ; the Nativity of Our Lady (Sept. 8th); the Exaltation of the Holy Cross (Sept. 14th); All-Saints (Nov. 1st); during the octave of All-Souls ; the Presentation of Our Lady (Nov. 21st).

2. One hundred days for every recitation of the prayer, "Chosen lily," &c. (Page 77.)

   The same Indulgence (*once a day*) for the recitation of the prayer, "My dear Jesus," &c. (Page 91).

3. Sixty days as often as the members accompany the holy Viaticum, or say an Our Father and Hail Mary for the sick, or an Our Father and Hail Mary for deceased members; as often as they restore peace between enemies, or perform any work of mercy; as often as they exercise any act of piety, or assist at the Holy Mass or other Christian assemblies for the honor of God; and lastly, as often as they say fifteen Hail Maries corresponding to the fifteen knots of the girdle, in order to obtain for themselves and all the members of the Confraternity the grace of purity of heart.

Conditions for becoming a member of the Confraternity of the Cord of St. Thomas of Aquin.

1. To be inscribed in the register of the Confraternity by a priest duly authorized by the Very Rev. General of the Dominicans.
2. Day and night to wear around the waist the girdle of the Confraternity, viz., a white linen cord with fifteen knots, blessed by a duly authorized priest. The members must also cultivate a special devotion toward the most pure Virgin and the Angelic Doctor. (All this, however, is not binding under pain of sin.)

3. All the members of the Angelic Militia should strive, likewise, to subdue the temptations of the evil one and the emotions of the flesh as quickly as possible; they should never utter an improper word, suffer immodest pictures in their dwellings, be present at spectacles or plays of doubtful morality, nor indulge in dancing, reading obscene literature, or singing impure songs; above all, they must shun the dangers arising from worldly pleasures, and be earnest and heedful in guarding the holy virtue of purity. The members must never tolerate anything improper in others and, whenever they can, they must bring their fellow-men back from the pernicious indulgence in carnal pleasures, and gently allure them to the practice of the angelic virtue.

(Taken from Statute I. of the Angelic Militia. Bolland. Act. Sanct. Mart. tom I.)

The daily recitation of the following indulgenced prayer, is recommended to the members.

Prayer to St. Thomas of Aquin for the Preservation of Innocence and Chastity.

Chosen lily of innocence, most chaste St. Thomas, thou who didst ever preserve thy baptismal robe unspotted, thou who wast by two angels girded, thou who wast thyself a true angel in the flesh, I intreat thee to recommend me to Jesus, the spotless Lamb, and to Mary, the Queen of Virgins, that wearing around my loins thy holy girdle which was granted thee as a pledge of thy purity, and imitating thy virtues upon earth, I may one day be crowned with thee, O thou powerful protector of my innocence!

Our Father. Hail Mary. Glory be to the Father.

V. Pray for us, O St. Thomas!

R. That we may be made worthy of the promises of Christ.

Let us pray.

O God, who didst deign to arm us with the girdle of St. Thomas in the assaults made upon our innocence, grant to our earnest prayers that we, under his heavenly protection, the impure enemy of our body and soul in this warfare may happily overcome; and adorned with the unfading lily of purity, in the midst of the angelic host, may receive the palm of celestial bliss. Through Christ our Lord. Amen.

(Ind. 100 days each time.)

HYMNS

OF

St. Thomas of Aquin to the Most Blessed Sacrament of the Altar.

I. Lauda Sion.

Lauda, Sion, Salvatorem,
Lauda Ducem, et Pastorem,
In hymnis, et canticis.
Quantum potes, tantum aude:
Quia major omni laude,
Nec laudare sufficis.

Laudis thema specialis,
Panis vivus, et vitalis,
Hodie proponitur.
Quem in sacrae mensa coenae,
Turbae fratrum, duodenae
Datum non ambigitur.

Sit laus plena, sit sonora,
Sit jucunda, sit decora
Mentis jubilatio.
Dies enim solemnis agitur,
In qua mensae prima recolitur
Hujus institutio.

In hac mensa novi Regis,
Novum Pascha novae Legis,
Phase vetus terminat.
Vetustatem novitas,
Umbram fugat veritas,
Noctem lux eliminat.

Quod in coena Christus gessit,
Faciendum hoc expressit
In sui memoriam.
Docti sacris institutis,
Panem, vinum in salutis
Consecramus hostiam.

Dogma datur Christianis,
Quod in carnem transit panis,
Et vinum in sanguinem.
Quod non capis, quod non vides,
Animosa firmat fides,
Praeter rerum ordinem.

Sub diversis speciebus,
Signis tantum, et non rebus,
Latent res eximiae.
Caro cibus, sanguis potus,
Manet tamen Christus totus
Sub utraque specie.

A sumente non concisus,
Non confractus, non divisus,
Integer accipitur.
Sumit unus, sumunt mille:
Quantum iste, tantum ille:
Nec sumptus consumitur.

Sumunt boni, sumunt mali,
Sorte tamen inaequali,
Vitae vel interitus.
Mors est malis, vita bonis:
Vide, paris sumptionis,
Quam sit dispar exitus.

Fracto demum Sacramento,
Ne vacilles, sed memento,
Tantum esse sub fragmento,
Quantum toto tegitur.

Nulla rei fit scissura:
Signi tantum fit fractura,
Qua nec status, nec statura
Signati minuitur.

Ecce panis Angelorum,
Factus cibus viatorum,
Vere panis filiorum,
Non mittendus canibus.

In figuris praesignatur,
Cum Isaac immolatur
Agnus Paschae deputatur
Datur manna patribus.

Bone Pastor, panis vere,
Jesu nostri miserere;
Tu nos pasce, nos tuere,
Tu nos bona fac videre
In terra viventium.

Tu qui cuncta scis, et vales,
Qui nos pascis hic mortales,
Tuos ibi commensales,
Cohaeredes et sodales
Fac Sanctorum civium. Amen.

TRANSLATION OF THE "LAUDA SION."

(From Caswell's "*Lyra Catholica*").

Sion, lift thy voice and sing;
Praise thy Saviour and thy king;
  Praise with hymns thy Shepherd true:
Strive thy best to praise Him well;
Yet doth He all praise excel;
  None can ever reach His due.

See to-day before us laid
The living and life-giving Bread,
  Theme for praise and joy profound!
The same which at the sacred board
Was, by our Incarnate Lord,
  Given to His Apostles round.

Let the praise be loud and high;
Sweet and tranquil be the joy
  Felt to-day in every breast;
On this festival divine,
Which records the origin
  Of the glorious Eucharist.

On this Table of the King,
Our new Paschal offering
  Brings to end the olden rite;
Here for empty shadows fled,
Is Reality instead;
  Here instead of darkness Light.

His own act at supper seated,
Christ ordained to be repeated,
   In His Memory divine;
Wherefore now with adoration,
We the Host of our salvation
   Consecrate from bread and wine.

Hear what Holy Church maintaineth,
That the bread its substance changeth
   Into Flesh, the wine to Blood.
Doth it pass thy comprehending?
Faith, the law of sight transcending,
   Leaps to things not understood.

Here beneath these signs are hidden
Priceless things to sense forbidden;
   Signs, not things, are all we see:—
Flesh from bread, and Blood from wine;
Yet is Christ in either sign,
   All entire confessed to be.

They, too, who of Him partake,
Sever not nor rend nor break,
   But entire their Lord receive.
Whether one or thousands eat,
All receive the self-same meat,
   Nor the less for others leave.

Both the wicked and the good
Eat of this celestial Food;
   But with ends how opposite!
Here 'tis life; and there 'tis death;
The same, yet issuing to each
   In a difference infinite.

Not a single doubt retain,
When they break the host in twain,
But that in each part remains
   What was in the whole before;
Since the simple sign alone
Suffers change in state or form,
The Signified remaining One
   And the Same for evermore.

Lo! upon the altar lies,
Hidden deep from human eyes,
Bread of angels from the skies,
   Made the food of mortal man:
Children's meat to dogs denied;
In old types foresignified,
In the manna Heaven supplied,
   Isaac, and the Paschal Lamb.

Jesus, Shepherd of the sheep!
Thou Thy flock in safety keep.
Living Bread! Thy life supply;
Strengthen us, or else we die;
   Fill us with celestial grace;
Thou who feedest us below,
Source of all we have or know,
Grant that with Thy saints above,
Sitting at the feast of love,
   We may see Thee face to face!

---

2. Sacris Solemniis Juncta Sint Gaudia.

Sacris solemniis juncta sint gaudia
Et ex praecordiis sonent praeconia,
Recedant vetera, nova sint omnia:
   Corda, voces, et opera.

Noctis recolitur coena novissima,
Qua Christus creditur agnum, et azyma
Dedisse fratribus, juxta legitima,
   Priscis indulta patribus.

Post agnum typicum, expletis epulis,
Corpus Dominicum datum discipulis,
Sic totum omnibus, quod totum singulis,
   Ejus fatemur manibus.

Dedit fragilibus Corporis ferculum,
Dedit et tristibus Sanguinis poculum,
Dicens: Accipite quod trado vasculum,
   Omnes ex eo bibite.

Sic sacrificium istud instituit,
Cujus officium committi voluit
Solis presbyteris, quibus sic congruit,
   Ut sumant, et dent ceteris.

Panis Angelicus fit panis hominum :
Dat panis coelicus figuris terminum :
O res mirabilis, manducat Dominum
　　Pauper, servus, et humilis.

Te, trina Deitas, unaque poscimus,
Sic nos tu visita, sicut te colimus,
Per tuas semitas duc nos quo tendimus,
　　Ad lucem, quam inhabitas.　Amen.

TRANSLATION OF "SACRIS SOLEMNIIS."

(From Caswell's "*Lyra Catholica*").

Let us with hearts renewed,
　Our grateful homage pay ;
And welcome with triumphant songs
　This ever-blessed day.

Upon this hallowed night
　Christ with His brethren ate,
Obedient to the Olden Law,
　The Pasch before Him set.

Which done,—Himself entire,
　The true Incarnate God,
Alike on each, alike on all,
　His sacred hands bestowed.

He gave His Flesh ; He gave
　His precious Blood ; and said,
"Receive, and drink ye all of this,
　For your salvation shed."

Thus did the Lord appoint
　This Sacrifice sublime,
And made His priests Its ministers
　Through all the bounds of time.

Farewell to types! Henceforth
　We feed on angel's food :
The guilty slave—oh, wonder!—eats
　The Body of his God!

O Blessed three in One!
　Visit our hearts, we pray ;
And lead us on through Thine own paths
　To Thy eternal day!

3. Verbum Supernum.

Verbum supernum prodiens,
Nec Patris linquens dexteram
Ad opus suum exiens,
Venit ad vitae vesperam.

In mortem a discipulo
Suis tradendus aemulis,
Prius in vitae ferculo
Se tradidit discipulis.

Quibus sub bina specie
Carnem dedit et sanguinem,
Ut duplicis substantiae
Totum cibaret hominem.

Se nascens dedit socium,
Convescens in edulium,
Se moriens in pretium,
Se regnans dat in praemium.

O salutaris Hostia,
Quae coeli pandis ostium:
Bella premunt hostilia,
Da robur, fer auxilium.

Uni, trinoque Domino,
Sit sempiterna gloria:
Qui vitam sine termino
Nobis donet in patria. Amen.

TRANSLATION OF "VERBUM SUPERNUM."

(From Caswell's "*Lyra Catholica*").

The Word, descending from above,
  Though with the Father still on high,
Went forth upon His work of love,
  And soon to life's last eve drew nigh.

He shortly to a death accursed
  By a disciple shall be given;
But to His twelve disciples first
  He gives Himself, the Bread from heaven.

Himself in either kind He gave:
   He gave His Flesh, He gave His Blood;
Of flesh and blood all men are made;
   And He of man would be the Food.

At birth our brother He became;
   At board Himself as food He gives;
To ransom us He died in shame;
   As our reward in bliss He lives.

O saving victim! opening wide
   The gate of heaven to man below!
Our foes press on from every side;—
   Thine aid supply, Thy strength bestow.

To Thy great Name be endless praise,
   Immortal Godhead, one in Three!
Oh, grant us endless length of days,
   In our true native land with Thee!

---

4. Pange, Lingua.

Pange, lingua, gloriosi
Corporis mysterium,
Sanguinisque pretiosi,
Quem in mundi pretium
Fructus ventris generosi,
Rex effudit gentium.

Nobis datus, nobis natus
Ex intacta Virgine,
Et in mundo conversatus,
Sparso verbi semine,
Sui moras incolatus
Miro clausit ordine.

In supremae nocte coenae
Recumbens cum fratribus.
Observata lege plene
Cibis in legalibus,
Cibum turbae duodenae
Se dat suis manibus.

Verbum caro, panem verum
Verbo carnem efficit:
Fitque sanguis Christi merum,
Etsi sensus deficit,
Ad firmandum cor sincerum
Sola fides sufficit.

Tantum ergo Sacramentum
Veneremur cernui:
Et antiquum documentum
Novo cedat ritui:
Praestet fides supplementum
Sensuum defectui.

Genitori, Genitoque
Laus, et jubilatio,
Salus, honor, virtus quoque
Sit, et benedictio:
Procedenti ab utroque
Compar sit laudatio. Amen.

TRANSLATION OF "PANGE, LINGUA."

(From Caswell's *Lyra Catholica.*)

Sing, my tongue, the Saviour's glory,
  Of His Flesh the mystery sing;
Of the Blood, all price exceeding,
  Shed by our Immortal King,
Destined, for the world's redemption,
  From a noble womb to spring.

Of a pure and spotless Virgin
  Born for us on earth below,
He, as Man with man conversing,
  Stayed, the seeds of truth to sow;
Then He closed in solemn order
  Wondrously His life of woe.

On the night of that Last Supper,
  Seated with His chosen band,
He the Paschal victim eating,
  First fulfils the Law's command;
Then as Food to all His brethren
  Gives Himself with His own hand.

Word made Flesh, the bread of nature
   By His word to Flesh He turns;
Wine into His Blood He changes:—
   What though sense no change discerns?
Only be the heart in earnest,
   Faith her lesson quickly learns.

Down in adoration falling,
   Lo! the Sacred Host we hail;
Lo! o'er ancient forms departing,
   Newer rites of grace prevail;
Faith for all defects supplying,
   Where the feeble senses fail.

To the Everlasting Father,
   And the Son, who reigns on high,
With the Holy Ghost proceeding
   Forth from Each eternally,
Be salvation, honor, blessing,
   Might and endless majesty.

5. Adoro Te.

Adoro te devote, latens Deitas,
Quae sub his figuris vere latitas;
Tibi se cor meum totum subjicit,
Quia te contemplans, totum deficit.

Visus, gustus, tactus, in te fallitur,
Sed auditu solo tuto creditur.
Credo quidquid dixit Dei Filius,
Nil hoc verbo veritatis verius.

In cruce latebat sola Deitas,
At hic latet simul et humanitas:
Ambo tamen credens atque confitens,
Peto, quod petivit latro poenitens.

Plagas, sicut Thomas non intueor.
Deum tamen meum te confiteor.
Fac me tibi semper magis credere,
In te spem habere, te diligere.

O memoriale mortis Domini,
Panis vivus, vitam praestans homini:
Praesta meae menti de te vivere:
Et te illi semper dulce sapere.

Pie pellicane, Jesu Domine,
Me immundum munda tuo sanguine,
Cujus una stilla salvum facere,
Totum mundum quit ab omni scelere.

Jesu, quem velatum nunc aspicio,
Oro, fiat illud, quod tam sitio;
Ut te revelata cernens facie,
Visu sim beatus tuae gloriae. Amen.

TRANSLATION OF "ADORO TE."

(From Caswell's "*Lyra Catholica*").

O Godhead hid, devoutly I adore Thee,
Who truly art within the forms before me;
To Thee my heart I bow with bended knee,
As failing quite in contemplating Thee.

Sight, touch, and taste in Thee are all deceived;
The ear alone most safely is believed:
I believe all the Son of God has spoken,
Than Truth's own word there is no truer token.

God only on the Cross lay hid from view;
But here lies hid at once the Manhood too;
And I in both professing my belief,
Make the same prayer as the repentant thief.

Thy wounds as Thomas saw, I do not see;
Yet Thee confess my Lord and God to be;
Make me believe Thee ever more and more;
In Thee my hope, in Thee my love to store.

O Thou, Memorial of our Lord's own dying!
O living Bread, to mortals life supplying!
Make Thou my soul henceforth on Thee to live;
Ever a taste of heavenly sweetness give.

O loving Pelican! O Jesu, Lord!
Unclean I am, but cleanse me in Thy blood,
Of which a single drop for sinners spilt,
Can purge the entire world from all its guilt.

Jesus! whom for the present veiled I see,
What I so thirst for, oh, vouchsafe to me!
That I may see Thy countenance unfolding,
And may be blessed Thy glory in beholding.

(The following is usually sung after every stanza.)

Jesu, Eternal Shepherd! hear our cry;
Increase the faith of all whose souls on Thee rely!

SOME PRAYERS

OF

ST. THOMAS OF AQUIN.

PRAYER FOR THE PRESERVATION OF CHASTITY.

(St. Thomas first utterd this prayer after the wonderful victory that secured to him at one and the same time his vocation and his chastity, and won for him the title "Angel of the Schools").

My dear Jesus, I well know that every perfect gift, and above all others, the gift of chastity depends upon the powerful influence of Thy grace, and that without Thee no creature can do anything. I pray Thee, therefore, to protect with Thy grace the chastity and purity of my soul and body. And should I experience in myself a sensual impression, that could sully chastity and purity, do Thou banish it from me, O Thou who art the supreme Lord of all the powers of my soul, that with a spotless heart I may walk in Thy love and service, whilst every day of my life I sacrifice myself pure and chaste upon the most pure altar of Thy Divinity! Amen.

(See the Indulgence granted to the members of the Confraternity of the Cord of St. Thomas of Aquin, page 74.)

PRAYER BEFORE HOLY COMMUNION.

O Almightly and Eternal God, behold I draw near to the Sacrament of Thy only-begotten Son, our Lord Jesus Christ! I come as infirm to the Physician of life, as unclean to the fountain of mercy, as blind to the light of eternal splendor, as poor and needy to the Lord of heaven and earth. I implore the abundance of Thy immense bounty that Thou wouldst deign to cure my infirmity, to wash away my uncleanness, to enlighten my blindness, to enrich my poverty, to clothe my nakedness, that I may receive the Bread of angels, the King of kings, the Lord of hosts, with so great reverence and humility, with such contrition and devotion, such purity and faith, with that purpose and intention as is profitable to the salvation of my soul. Grant me, I beseech Thee, not only to receive the Sacrament of the Body and Blood of the Lord, but also the essence and virtue of the Sacrament! O most mild God, grant that the Body of Thy only-begotten Son, our Lord Jesus Christ, which He took from the Virgin Mary, I may so receive as to deserve to be incorporated with His mystical Body and to be numbered among His members! O most loving Father, grant that Thy Beloved Son, whom now in life I am about to receive veiled, I may perpetually contemplate revealed face to face! Who liveth and reigneth with Thee in the unity of the Holy Ghost one God forever and ever. Amen.

PRAYER AFTER HOLY COMMUNION.

I give Thee thanks, O holy Lord, Almighty Father, Eternal God, who hast deigned, through no merits of mine, but only through Thy own mercy, to feed me, a sinner, Thy unworthy servant, with the precious Body and Blood of Thy

Son, our Lord Jesus Christ. And I pray that this Holy Communion may not be for me a subject for punishment, but a salutary pleading for pardon. May it be to me the armor of faith and the shield of good will! May it be the extirpation of my vices, and the increase of charity and patience, of humility and obedience, and of all the virtues; a firm defence against the snares of all enemies, visible and invisible; a perfect quieting of all my affections, both carnal and spiritual; a firm adhesion to Thee, the one and true God, and the blessed consummation of my end. And I pray Thee to deign to lead me a sinner, to that ineffable banquet where Thou with Thy Son and the Holy Spirit, art the true light, the full plenitude, the everlasting joy, the consummate delight, the perfect felicity of Thy saints. Through the same Christ, our Lord. Amen.

PRAYER OF ST. THOMAS TO THE BLESSED VIRGIN MARY.

O most blessed, most sweet Virgin Mary, Mother of God, Daughter of the Most High King, Mistress of the angels, and Mother of all the faithful! O thou who art full of all blessings, into the bosom of thy goodness I commend now and all the rest of my life, my body, my soul, all my actions, my thoughts, desires, intentions, words, works, my whole life and my death, that all through thy intercession, and conformably to the will of thy Beloved Son, our Lord Jesus Christ, may tend to God. O be thou to me, my blessed Mistress, a helper and consoler in the snares and attacks of the old enemy and of all my adversaries! Of thy beloved Son, our Lord Jesus Christ, obtain for me, I beseech thee, the grace valiantly to resist the temptations of the world, the flesh, and the devil, and ever to persevere in the firm resolution never more to sin, but to be faithful in thy service and that of thy dear Son! I earnestly pray thee, my most holy Mistress, to obtain for me true obedience and true humility of heart, in order that I may acknowledge myself a weak and miserable sinner, unfit, not only to do anything good, but even to resist continued assaults without the help and grace of my Creator and thy holy prayers. Obtain for me also, O my sweetest Mistress, perpetual chastity of soul and body, that, with a pure heart and chaste body, I may serve thy beloved Son and thee in my state of life (in my Order). Obtain for me voluntary poverty, patience, and peace of soul with which to endure the pains of my state (my Order), and labor at my own and my neighbor's salvation. Obtain for me also, O sweetest Mistress, true love with which I may love thy holy Son, our Lord Jesus Christ, with my whole heart, and then thee above all others, and afterward my neighbor in God and for God, that I may rejoice in his welfare and mourn over his misfortunes, that I may not despise nor insolently censure any-one, nor in my heart prefer myself to anyone. Obtain also, O Queen of Heaven, that I may have in my breast fear as well as love for thy sweetest Son; that I may thank Him always for the benefits which, through no merit of my own, but out of His own pure goodness, He has bestowed upon me; that I may sincerely confess my sins and do true penance for them, that I may thereby be worthy to receive His mercy and grace. I beg thee, also, O my incomparable Mother, thou gate of heaven and mediatrix of sinners, not to suffer me, thy unworthy servant, at the close of my life to fall away from the holy, Catholic faith; but in thy great goodness and mercy, come to my aid and defend me from the evil spirits. Infuse into my soul hope in the blessings flowing from the glorious Passion of thy Son and in thy own mediation; implore Him to grant me forgiveness of my sins, and conduct me, when I die in His love and thine, on the way of deliverance and salvation. Amen.

PRAYER OF ST. THOMAS.

Frequently used by him before dictating, writing or preaching.

Ineffable Creator, Thou who out of the treasures of Thy wisdom, didst form three hierarchies of angels and set them over the radiant heavens in wonderful order; Thou who didst dispose all parts of the universe with so great magnificence; Thou who art called the true Source of light and wisdom, the Supreme Fountain of all things; deign to shed a ray of Thy splendor over the darkness of my understanding, and thereby remove the twofold night wherein I was born; viz., the night of sin and the night of ignorance. O Thou who canst make eloquent the tongues of little ones, form my tongue and pour out upon my lips the grace of Thy blessing! Give me keenness of intelligence and power of retaining, capacity to receive instruction, penetration to expound, and abundant grace to speak. Do thou direct me in the beginning, conduct me in the progress, and at the close supply for the deficiencies of all my undertakings. Thou who livest and reignest true God and Man for ever and ever. Amen.

(His Holiness Leo XIII., under date of Feb. 21, 1880, to all that devoutly recite this prayer, granted an Indulgence of 200 days, to be gained once a day.)

A SHORT PRAYER WHICH ST. THOMAS SAID DAILY KNEELING.

Concede mihi, quaeso, misericors Deus, quae tibi sunt placita, ardenter concupiscere, prudenter investigare, veraciter agnoscere, et perfecte implere, ad laudem et gloriam Nominis tui. Amen.

Grant me, I beseech Thee, O merciful God! ardently to desire, prudently to investigate, truly to acknowledge, and perfectly to fulfil that which is pleasing to Thee, to the praise and glory of Thy Name. Amen.

(On June 29, 1878, Leo XIII., granted an Indulgence of 300 days to all that, with a contrite heart, recite this prayer before study or reading.)

DAILY PRAYER OF ST. THOMAS

Before a Picture of Christ to obtain a Holy and Perfect Life.

Grant me, I beseech Thee, almighty and merciful God, to desire fervently, to investigate wisely, to acknowledge sincerely, and to fulfil perfectly the things that please Thee. Dispose my state of life to the praise and glory of Thy Name. Give me the knowledge, ability, and will, to do what Thou requirest of me; and grant me grace to perform it well, to the advancement of my soul's salvation.

Let my way to Thee, I beseech Thee, be safe, direct, and perfect, not failing either in prosperity or adversity; but leaving me undepressed by the one, and unelated by the other. Let me thank Thee in prosperity, and preserve my patience in adversity. Let me be glad or sorry for nothing, except it carry me on to Thee, or draw me back from Thee. Let me seek to please and fear to displease none but Thee.

Grant that I may do all things in charity and count for dead whatever has nothing to do with Thy service. Grant that I may not perform my actions from custom, but with devotion for an offering to Thee.

Let all that is transitory be worthless to me for Thy sake, and all that is Thine precious; but Thou, my God, more precious than all. Let every labor that is for Thee delight me, and all repose that is not in Thee be wearisome to me. Enable me, dearest Lord, to turn my heart to Thee frequently and fervently, and to atone for my faults by sorrow with purpose of amendment. Make me, O my God, humble without pretence, merry without dissipation, sorrowful without dejection, sedate without moroseness, active without levity, truthful without duplicity, timid without despair, hopeful in Thee without presumption, chaste without taint. Enable me to reprove my neighbor without displeasure, and edify him by word and example without pride; to be obedient without contradiction, and patient without murmuring.

Give me, dearest Jesus, a watchful heart that is not led away from Thee by curious thoughts; a steadfast heart that is dragged down from Thee by no unworthy affection; a dauntless heart that is tired out by no tribulation; a free heart that is enslaved by no pleasure of passion; and an upright heart that is turned aside by no sinister intention. Bestow upon me, my dearest Lord, understanding to know Thee; diligence to seek Thee; wisdom to find Thee; such a way of living as to please Thee; perseverance, sweetly and confidently to await Thee and, at last, to attain to Thee. Grant me by penance to share in Thy sufferings; by grace to enjoy Thy blessings on my way to Thee, and by glory at last to possess Thy delights in my heavenly country. Who with the Father and the Holy Ghost, livest and reignest God, world without end. Amen.

PRAYER OF ST. THOMAS TO OBTAIN THE VIRTUES.

Almighty God, Thou who knowest all things, Thou who art without beginning or end, Thou who dost bestow, preserve, and reward the virtues, vouchsafe to confirm me in the firm foundation of faith, to protect me with the indestructible shield of hope, and to adorn me with the wedding garment of charity. Grant that in justice I may be subject to Thee, that with prudence I may shun the snares of the evil one, and with fortitude patiently endure adversity. Grant that I may freely share what I have with those that have not, and that what I myself have not I may humbly seek from those that have. Grant that the guilt I have committed, I may sincerely confess, and the punishment I endure, I may bear with equanimity. Grant that I may not envy my neighbor his goods, and that I may always thank Thee for Thy gifts. In rest and motion, may I be always reserved! May I preserve my tongue from vainglorious words, guard my feet from transgressing, restrain my eyes from wandering glances, withdraw my ears from the noise of the world, incline my head humbly, lift up my mind to heavenly things, despise what is transient, long only after Thee, subdue my flesh, purify my conscience, honor the saints, praise Thee worthily, increase in blessings, and end my good works by a holy death! Implant in me, O Lord, the virtues, that I may be toward holy things devout, in earthly duties prudent, in my behaviour troublesome to no one. Give me, O Lord, heartfelt repentance, sincere confession, and the grace to make perfect satisfaction. Vouchsafe that I may so regulate my interior by a good life, that I may do what is becoming, what will redound to my own merit, and be for the edification of my neighbor. Grant that I may never aim after anything foolish, or from distaste omit what is repulsive to me; that thereby I may not desire before the time that which is not yet begun, nor long to give up before it is finished what has been begun. Amen.

Letter of St. Thomas of Aquin to a Novice,

upon the proper way to attain divine, as well as human wisdom.

As you have inquired of me, John, dearly beloved in Christ, how you should study, in order to obtain the treasure of wisdom, I now give you the counsel not to plunge at once into the sea, but first into the little brook, because one must go from easier to more difficult things. Hearken now to my counsel for your instruction. Be reserved in speech and seldom go to the parlor. Apply yourself to purity of conscience. Cease not to pray. Love your cell dearly, if you desire to be introduced into the wine cellar of the Beloved. Be amiable to all, and do not vex yourself at the doings of others. Be not too confidential to any one, because too great intimacy begets contempt, and will be the occasion of estrangement from study. Do not mix yourself up with the sayings and doings of worldlings. Above all, refrain from strolling around. Neglect not to tread in the footsteps of the saints and good people. Consider not who it is that speaks; but the good that he utters, impress upon thy memory. Try to understand whatever you read and hear. In doubts, endeavor to arrive at the solution; and as far as you can, seek to store your mind, like one that wishes to fill a vessel. Strive not after what is too high for you.

If you follow these hints, you will, during your whole life, bring forth and ripen many flowers and fruits in the vineyard of the Lord of hosts. If you practise them, you will attain the object of your desires. Farewell!

CRUX ANGELICA.

In cruce est perfectio totius legis, et tota ars bene vivendi. (S. Thom. in Ep. ad Gal. cap. VI, lect. 4.
(In the cross is the perfecting of the whole law, and the whole science of living well.)

Crux mihi certa salus — Crux est quam semper adoro — Crux Domini mecum — Crux mihi refugium

Crux mihi certa salus, crux est quam semper adoro;
Crux Domini mecum, crux mihi refugium.

It was in this form that St. Thomas himself drew a cross on the wall of St. James's church at Anagni. Pope Pius IX. granted under date of Jan. 21, 1876, to all the faithful, once a day, an Indulgence of 300 days for the devout recital of the verses:

> "The cross is my sure salvation, the cross will I always adore.
> May the cross of my Lord be about me! be my refuge forevermore!"

THE DAILY EXERCISES OF A CHRISTIAN.

(From Father von Cochem's "Little Myrtle Garden".)

MORNING PRAYERS.

1. To God the Father.

O most holy, heavenly Father! I raise my heart and soul to Thee at early morn; and, as a token of my filial love, I send up my sighs and prayers to Thee in heaven.

Prostrate at the feet of Thy divine Majesty, I adore Thy infinite Divinity, and give Thee thanks for graciously granting me another day in which to work out my salvation. I am Thy creature. To Thee am I indebted for my existence and its continued preservation; therefore am I obliged to serve Thee, and for Thee alone, O my Creator and Supreme Lord, to live. As a morning sacrifice well-pleasing to Thee, I offer Thee my heart, the noblest gift in my power to bestow, a gift that I first received from Thee. My soul sighs for nothing but to love Thee, to increase ever more and more in Thy love, and to perform all the works of this day for Thy greater glory alone. Amen.

2. To Jesus Christ.

I adore Thee, O my Crucified Saviour, and give Thee heartfelt thanks that Thou didst deign to die on the cross for me and through Thy bitter Passion to open anew to me the Paradise that sin had lost! To make some return for so great a benefit, I am firmly resolved to serve Thee to-day with filial love and fidelity, and to perform all my actions to honor Thy bitter Passion and death.

As Thou when hanging on the cross, by the laceration of Thy sacred members, didst operate my salvation, so do I desire to-day to use all the members of my body and all the powers of my soul in Thy sweet service and in honor of those immense sufferings which Thou didst endure on the cross for me! Amen.

3. To the Holy Ghost.

I adore Thee, O beneficent Holy Spirit! I bless Thy divine mercy that has added another day to my life. I accept it as a special grace from Thy divine hand, and I will make use of it so to honor the bitter Passion of my Lord and Saviour that I may rejoice for all eternity for having lived to see it.

Thou, O Holy Spirit, O Spirit of Love, thou art the Fountain-head of all graces! I pray Thee, therefore, to bestow upon me the grace to keep my soul free from sin to-day and to think often upon the bitter Passion of my Lord. Amen.

4. Good Intentions for the Day.

O my God, I solemnly promise before Thee and the whole heavenly court, to serve Thee to-day with all my strength, and to perform all my actions for Thy good pleasure!

With the same intention that animated Christ and all the saints, I desire to perform all my spiritual and corporal works, offering them to Thee in the most perfect manner.

I unite all my thoughts, words, and actions to the most holy thoughts, words, and actions of my Saviour Jesus Christ and all the saints. I desire to become as pleasing to Thee by my works as the saints did by theirs whilst on earth. Amen.

Contract with Christ.

(To be renewed every week.)

O my true Redeemer, Jesus Christ! since no exercise of devotion is more pleasing to Thee than those that are made in honor of Thy bitter Passion, I am resolved frequently to reflect thereon.

As often as I glance toward heaven, I will call to mind how frequently Thou didst raise Thine eyes to implore Thy Father's aid during Thy Passion.

As often as I cast my eyes down, I will recall the lowering of Thy eyes during Thy Passion when, through shame, Thou didst not dare to fix them on anyone.

As often as I draw my breath, I will recall how often Thou didst sigh during Thy Passion and make known Thy sufferings to Thy Father.

As often as I move my hands, I will do it in memory of the thousands of blows Thou didst receive in Thy Passion; and as often as I take a step I will offer it in honor of the bloody steps Thou didst then take.

At every mouthful that I eat, at every drop that I drink, I wish to thank Thee a thousand times for the consuming thirst Thou didst suffer, for the gall and the vinegar Thou didst taste during Thy bitter Passion.

With the bloody sweat that thou didst pour out for me in the Garden of Olives and on the holy Cross when Thou didst struggle in Thy bitter death agony, I will mingle every drop of mine, telling Thee a thousand and a thousand times that I thank Thee!

And lastly, at every pulsation of my heart, at every throb of my pulse, I will thank Thee, O my dearest Lord, for all the agony of Thy Sacred Heart, for all the mortal wounds It received during Thy bitter Passion!

O Jesus, deign to ratify this covenant and receive it from me with the intention of renewing it at every moment. I wish to perform all my actions as stated in this contract.

This is my most earnest intention, in which I desire to persevere till the close of my life; viz, by every movement of my soul and body to render praise and thanksgiving for Thy bitter Passion. Amen.

EVENING PRAYERS.

1. *To the Most Holy Trinity.*

In the deepest humility, I bend my knee before Thee, O Most Holy Trinity, and at the close of this day lift up my soul to Thee, adoring Thee from the bottom of my heart!

For all the benefits I have to-day received from Thee, be Thou eternally blessed! and for the paternal care with which Thou hast preserved me from many sins and evils, be Thou forever praised and adored! But since I can not praise Thee worthily, may the nine choirs of angels and the multitude of the elect thank and glorify Thee for me! Whatever good I have done this day and have forgotten to offer to Thee, I now present to Thee, desiring with my whole heart that all and everything which I have to-day done and suffered may tend to Thy greatest glory.

I commend myself anew to Thy paternal care and divine protection, that the wicked enemy may do me no harm to-night in body or soul, but that, to Thy honor, I may rest in peace. Amen.

Here examine your conscience upon the faults of the whole day. Excite your soul to compunction whilst saying:—

O my crucified Jesus! in the sorrow of my heart I prostrate before Thee. I bewail my fault of having served Thee so negligently this day and offended Thee by so many sins.

I firmly resolved this morning carefully to avoid all sin; but I forgot my good intention, I have deeply offended and irritated Thee by my numerous sins, by my negligence. Pardon me, O my Jesus, and in the ruby stream of Thy Precious Blood wash away all the stains by which I have disfigured my soul. I implore Thee by the tortures and pains which, in Thy bitter Passion and especially on the cross, Thou didst endure, that Thou wouldst disarm the just anger of Thy Father against me, make satisfaction to Him for the punishment I so well deserve, and obtain for me the grace to serve Thee better for the future and ever to increase in Thy divine love. Amen.

2. To the Blessed Virgin.

Loving Virgin Mary, I remind thee of the night after that thrice-blessed day which we call Good-Friday, and which thou must have spent in deep anguish of heart separated from thy dear Son. Through the bitter sighs and tears that thou didst then pour forth, I beg thee to help me to spend this night in honor of thy sorrowful night, and let me not forget the Passion of thy Son. Unite my every respiration to thine own sighs of sorrow, every pulsation of my heart to the grief and distress of thine own, and offer them all to thy Crucified Son in honor of His Passion and in thanksgiving for all that He has obtained for us by it. Amen.

3. To the Guardian Angel.

I, thy unworthy child, salute thee, my dear angel, and thank thee for the love and fidelity thou hast shown me to-day. O my holy angel, how can I thank thee for all thy love and care in guarding me from evil! Unthankful child that I am, I not only neglect thy inspirations, but still more grieve thee by my daily sins and imperfections. I pray thee, by the sorrowful Passion of our Lord Jesus Christ, pardon me for having so often offended thee, and obtain for me the grace to amend my sinful life. Preserve me this night from all the snares of Satan and from a sudden and unprovided death. Receive my every respiration, every throb of my pulse, and offer them to my Crucified Jesus in honor of His bitter Passion and death. Amen.

4. *The Good Intention for the Night.*

O Lord Jesus Christ, in honor of Thy most painful sleep upon the hard wood of the cross, when Thou didst bow Thy head in death, I now betake myself to rest, and in memory of Thy most bitter death I will fall asleep. Ah, what a hard bed, what a rough pillow Thou didst have when, wounded and bleeding, Thou didst hang upon the cross, Thy sacred head resting upon the thorny crown! For three long hours didst Thou hang in those cruel torments before, bowing Thy head, Thou didst give up Thy spirit and sleep the sleep of death! By that most bitter sleep, grant that my sleep may be directed to Thy honor and that no effort of the evil one may lead me into sin.

As St. John rested his head upon Thy sacred breast and thereon tasted the sweetest, the most blissful repose, so do I lay my sinful head upon Thy blessed breast and my lips upon Thy opened side, that my every respiration may enter into Thy Sacred Heart, and that I may thence draw into my own poor heart Thy sweetest love.

Sprinkling thyself and thy bed with holy water, say:

Visit, O Lord, this little bed of mine with Thy grace and drive far from it the snares of the enemy. May Thy holy angels watch over me and keep me in peace! May Thy blessing rest upon me and Thy divine love glow in my heart! Through Jesus Christ our Lord. Amen.

Then signing thyself with the sign of the cross, say:

May God the Father, God the Son, and God the Holy Ghost grant all that I have asked! Amen.

PRAYERS AT MASS.

Prayer upon Entering the Church.

I adore Thee, O my true Lord and God, dwelling in this holy temple, and I salute Thee as the Friend of my soul. I adore Thee, O Divine Sacrament of the Altar, and I firmly believe that my Lord Jesus Christ is really present in Thee. I bow my head most humbly and adore Thee. Dear saints, to whom this church and its altars are dedicated, and ye whose relics are here preserved, I salute you. I have come to visit you and implore your intercession. I unite in all the devotions and holy Masses that ever have been or that ever will be celebrated in this sacred building, that I may have a share in the blessings emanating from them. Amen.

A Devout Method of Assisting at the Holy Mass in Honor of the Bitter Passion of Our Lord Jesus Christ.

Prayer before Holy Mass.

O my Crucified Jesus, Thou who hast redeemed me from everlasting death by Thy own bitter Passion, I purpose now to assist devoutly at this Holy Mass in thanksgiving for all Thou hast done for me, reflecting at the same time upon Thy cruel sufferings!

For this end, grant me Thy grace and soften my hard heart, that I may feel the pains of what Thou hast endured and tenderly sympathize with Thee. I recommend to Thee myself and all my dear ones, that we may share in the blessings of this Holy Sacrifice, and I implore Thee to offer Thyself to Thy Heavenly Father for our salvation. Amen.

Here the priest and the server go up to the altar in imitation of Jesus and His disciples ascending Mount Olivet.

Prayer when the Priest goes up to the Altar.

Ah, my dearest Jesus, I behold Thee sorrowfully ascending the Mount of Olives with Thy disciples there to begin Thy bitter Passion and to implore mercy from Thy Heavenly Father for Thyself and for us! I unite with Thy loved disciples to bear Thee company, to share in Thy agony, and with Thee to call upon Thy Father.

When thou didst enter the garden of Gethsemane and Thy Father withdrew His sensible consolation, intense fear and sadness seized upon Thee. Then didst Thou with agonizing sighs exclaim:

"My soul is sorrowful even unto death!"—O my sorrowful Jesus, I sincerely compassionate Thee in Thy extreme affliction, which grieves me more than if it were my own! I will remain faithful to Thee in Thy sorrow, I will watch and pray near Thee; and do Thou, dearest Jesus, stay with me and let me share in Thy bitter chalice. Amen.

When the priest returns to the foot of the altar and begins the Holy Mass, imagine Christ separating from His disciples and praying to His Father to remove the chalice from Him. Impressed by the great suffering of thy Redeemer, say to Him with tender compassion:

Prayer when the Priest begins Holy Mass.

Most afflicted Jesus, in what a sea of sadness was Thy heart immersed when, leaving Thy beloved disciples, Thou didst go to the cave, to implore Thy Father's mercy! How humbly didst Thou fall upon Thy knees! how earnestly call upon Thy Father for help, saying: "My Father, if it be possible, let this chalice pass from Me. Neverthless not as I will, but as Thou wilt!"— And when Thy prayer was not granted, Thou didst fall in anguish upon Thy face, Thy heart beating violently with fear and dejection, Thy mental torture increasing, the cold sweat starting from every pore until, at the sight of Thy fearful sufferings, Thou didst fall into the agony of death, the bloody sweat oozing from Thy whole person and moistening the earth. O my Jesus! I implore Thee through the mortal agony Thou didst then endure, and through the bloody sweat Thou didst then pour forth, wash away the stains of my soul, and preserve me from dejection and despair when the hour of my own death draws near! Amen.

When the priest ascends the steps and kisses the altar, see Christ going to meet His enemies and receiving the kiss of perfidious Judas. In honor of this mystery, say the following:

Prayer when the Priest goes up to the Altar.

Remember, O my Jesus, how in Thy desire to suffer Thou didst go to meet Thy enemies and didst give to the betrayer Judas the kiss of a friend. Thy enemies fell upon Thee, cast Thee down rudely, bound Thee with ropes, and led Thee amid scorn and derision to the house of Annas, where Thou wast questioned concerning Thy doctrine and struck in Thy sacred face. I thank Thee, my sweetest Jesus, for the great love with which Thou didst suffer for me and receive that cruel blow. I pray Thee by Thy shameful captivity to free me from eternal imprisonment in hell, and lead me into the glorious city of the Heavenly Jerusalem! Amen.

When the priest goes to the middle of the altar, imagine Christ led to Caiaphas and found guilty of death, whilst the multitude cried out: "He is guilty of death!" In honor of that ignominy endured by Jesus, say the following:

Prayer at the Kyrie Eleison.

My good Jesus, be mindful of the intense confusion Thou didst endure when, abused, despised, and blasphemed, Thou wast led to Caiaphas. Ah, how many cruel blows, how much shameful derision didst Thou not endure on that night! I offer Thee all the scorn, all the pains Thou didst then suffer, and I beseech Thee to pardon Me for having so often offended and insulted Thee by my sins. Amen.

The Gloria is sometimes said, sometimes omitted. When it is said, thank Christ for the confusion that befell Him in the house of Caiaphas, and say:

Prayer at the Gloria.

I praise Thee, I extol Thee, I magnify Thee, O most faithful Redeemer Jesus Christ, and from the bottom of my heart I thank Thee for all the confusion offered Thee in the house of Caiaphas! As often as Thou wast blasphemed by the Jews, so many thousands of times do I bless Thee and give Thee thanks for the endurance of every outrage committed against Thee; for Thou alone art holy, Thou alone art worthy of praise, Thou alone art the Most High with the Holy Ghost in the glory of Thy Heavenly Father. Amen.

When the priest returns to the side of the altar, to read the Collect and Epistle, imagine thou seest Christ led to Pilate and falsely accused.

Prayer at the Collect and Epistle.

Be mindful, O my Jesus, of that sorrowful journey when, in the morning, Thou wast led from the house of Caiaphas to the palace of Pilate, there to be falsely accused by the populace, and to hear Thy death called for. Ah, what unspeakable confusion didst Thou endure when, bound with cords like a malefactor, Thou wast led through the midst of so many thousands of people and by them scorned and derided! They who once looked upon Thee as a holy prophet, regarded Thee now as an impious sinner; they raged violently against Thee, calling Thy virtues and miracles vices and sorcery. When they brought Thee to Pilate, they accused Thee as a seducer of the people. They cited false witnesses against Thee, and full of rage cried: "Away with Him! Crucify Him! Crucify Him!"—O my Jesus, how that murderous cry pierced Thy Heart and that of Thy Blessed Mother! What a pain to Thee and to her that they to whom Thou hadst done so much good, should repay Thee with so much suffering!

I pray Thee by that cruel clamoring for Thy life and the false accusations of the Jews, not to condemn me in accordance with my works when I stand before Thy judgment-seat justly accused by the evil one. By Thine own bitter sufferings, pronounce upon me a sentence of mercy. Amen.

When the priest goes to the other side of the altar to read the Gospel, see Christ led to Herod.

Prayer at the Gospel.

O Jesus, Thou meek Lamb, remember with what cruel derision Thou wast led to Herod, the godless king, accused by the high-priests, insulted by the soldiery, and like a fool clothed in a white garment. For all that derision and insult, I extol Thee in the name of all Thy creatures, whilst with heartfelt sorrow I call to mind my own deriding and transgressing of the wholesome lessons Thou hast given me in Thy holy Gospel. For these my manifold iniquities, O Jesus, I offer to Thy Father what Thou didst endure for me at the court of Herod. Amen.

After the Gospel, the priest returns to the middle of the altar, says the Credo and the prayers of the Offertory, and uncovers the chalice. All this signifies Christ led back from Herod to Pilate, again accused by the Jews, and at Pilate's command stripped and scourged.

Prayer at the Offertory.

O suffering Jesus, remember how, clothed in a white garment like a fool, Thou wast led back to Pilate through the assembled crowds. Again wast Thou falsely accused, stripped before the rabble, bound to a pillar, and cruelly scourged with rods and chains, until Thy whole body was one mass of wounds. But, like an innocent lamb, Thou didst stand at the pillar offering to Thy Father the cruel scourging and the bright red blood in satisfaction for sin and to repair His injured honor. Prostrate in spirit before Thee, I adore Thee, my mangled Redeemer! I kiss Thy wounded body and implore Thee, through this most fearful torture, to pardon my sins, especially those against holy purity. As Thou didst offer Thy bitter sufferings to Thy Father, and as the priest now offers to Thee bread and wine, so do I also offer Thee my body and soul, but more especially do I devote my heart to Thy service. I place my poor heart in the sacred chalice, and offer it to Thee by the hands of Thy minister. I offer Thee at the same time, in union with this holy Sacrifice of the Mass, all my crosses and difficulties, all my actions and cares. I put them all into the chalice and offer them up to Thee as my High Priest. Amen.

After the priest has poured wine into the chalice and raised it on high, he covers it with the pall and makes the sign of the cross over it. This signifies that Christ was crowned with thorns and struck in the face with the palm of the hand.

Prayer after the Offertory.

O Jesus, my bloody Spouse, who can ever truly feel what Thou didst endure when they crowned Thy royal head with thorns, driving them in so far as to increase the pain a hundred-fold, and to this torture adding that of striking Thy brow with a reed and Thy face with the palms of their hands! These cruel sufferings of Thine pierce my heart as once they pierced Thy sacred head. Offer them to Thy Heavenly Father and obtain for me the pardon of all the sins that I have committed by my head. Amen.

When the priest washes his hands, think of Pilate washing his after having uttered Christ's condemnation. See your Saviour laden with the cross and led out of Jerusalem.

Prayer at the Lavabo.

Now, O dearest Redeemer, is Thy life at an end, for Pilate has pronounced the unjust sentence that condemns Thee though innocent, to the death of the cross. I will follow Thee with heartfelt sympathy and bewail the ignominy with which Thou art led forth. I beseech Thee to send Thy holy angels to conduct my soul on its departure from this body. Amen.

When the priest turns and says the Orate Fratres, remember how Christ laden with the cross, turned and spoke to the daughters of Jerusalem.

Prayer at the Orate Fratres.

O Cross-bearer deserving of pity, Jesus Christ, Thou art now going forth to the most horrible torture, and yet Thy love for us is so great that Thou wishest to console in their sorrow the tearful daughters of Jerusalem, and once more to embrace in a sorrowful farewell Thy most afflicted Mother. O in what a sea of bitterness were immersed those loving hearts, Thine own and Thy most holy Mothers! Grant that I may share in Thy sufferings and let me never grow fainthearted under my own. Amen.

In the Preface the priest intones to God, the Lord, a hymn of praise and jubilation. The Church would thereby thank and praise Jesus Christ for enduring all the disgrace and ignominy offered Him by the Jews when He carried His cross.

Prayer at the Preface.

O my most faithful Redeemer, Jesus Christ! how great the insults and derision inflicted upon Thee when carrying Thy cross! how fearfully they abused Thee and blasphemed Thee! With ridicule and mockery they drove Thee from the city and dragged Thee like an infamous malefactor to the ignominious death of the cross. All this Thou didst endure patiently, nor didst Thou oppose a barrier to their scorn and blasphemy. In return for what Thou hast thus borne, I praise Thee, I bless Thee with Holy Mother Church; and since our praises are wholly inadequate, I call upon the nine choirs of angels to glorify Thee eternally, saying with them: Holy, holy, holy Lord God of

Sabaoth! Heaven and earth are full of the majesty of Thy glory! Hosanna in the highest!

After the Sanctus, the priest raises his hands and eyes to heaven, bows profoundly, kisses the altar, makes the sign of the cross three times over the chalice and the host. Imagine you see Jesus, after laying down His cross on Calvary, kneeling before it and, with hands and eyes raised to heaven, imploring His Father's assistance.

Prayer after the Sanctus.

O Jesus Christ, my Saviour! Then, indeed, did Thy sufferings begin when, fainting from pain and exhaustion, Thou didst reach Calvary's mount, there to be immolated like an innocent lamb. O God! what frightful tortures Thou didst then endure and how cruelly Thy executioners handled Thee! Ah, who would not pity Thee when, stripped of Thy garments Thou didst kneel at the side of Thy cross, to implore Thy Father to send Thee strength! And when Thy right hand had been cruelly pierced and nailed, Thy merciless executioners stretched Thy sacred body so violently that all Thy members were disjointed, Thy veins snapped and torn. And, at last, when Thy left hand and Thy feet were fastened to the cross, the agony was so intolerable as to force pitiful sighs and moans from Thy throbbing Heart.

O my Crucified Jesus! I fall in spirit on my knees before Thee and kiss the bleeding wounds of Thy sacred hands and feet. My heart is full of compassion for Thee and Thy immeasurable pains. Thy touching sighs are piercing my soul. Ah, my sins have caused all this suffering! I bewail them from the bottom of my heart and beg Thee, through the cruel torments of Thy Crucifixion, to pardon me and graciously remit my well-deserved chastisement. Amen.

The priest elevates the Sacred Host in remembrance of Jesus lifted up upon the cross.

Prayer at the Elevation of the Sacred Host.

I adore Thee, O my Crucified Jesus, and firmly believe that Thou art here present! O Jesus, be merciful to me, be propitious to me! O good Jesus, pardon my sins!

O Jesus Christ, Thou Mediator between God and man, as Thou didst hang upon the cross, Thou didst offer Thyself a sacrifice to Thy Father for the sins of the world! In the same manner, I now offer Thee anew for my own sins and those of the whole world. Preserve us from the just wrath of our Father in heaven, and obtain for us grace and mercy.

O Heavenly Father, look upon Thy beloved Son whom I offer to Thee for myself and all belonging to me, for all the living and the dead. Amen.

When the priest elevates the chalice, imagine you see Jesus' blood flowing down the cross from all the pores of His body, but especially from His hands and feet.

Prayer at the Elevation of the Chalice.

I adore Thee, O Precious Blood of my dear Redeemer Jesus Christ, and I firmly believe that Thou art here present! O holy Blood, wash me from every stain of sin! O ruby stream, remit my well deserved punishment! O Blood, rich in graces, obtain for me the grace and mercy of my

God! Heavenly Father, I offer Thee all the drops of this Precious Blood together with the love and anguish that drew them forth for the cleansing of my soul and for the ransom of the poor souls in purgatory. Amen.

The priest now prays in silence in memory of Jesus' hanging on the cross, like an innocent lamb not opening His mouth. As Jesus Christ is now truly, really, and essentially present on the altar, go stand before Him, as if you saw Him hanging upon the cross, and pour out thy whole heart to Him.

Prayer after the Elevation.

My Crucified Jesus, present now in body and soul upon this altar, I bend my knee before Thee in humble adoration! Like the penitent Magdalen, I embrace in spirit Thy holy cross. Remember, O Jesus, how Thou didst hang upon it, think of the superhuman pains Thou didst endure in all Thy members, of the ardor with which Thou didst intercede with Thy Father for sinners, how Thou didst offer for them Thy wounds and Thy Precious Blood! Since Thou art again our Mediator in this Holy Mass, I beseech Thee to intercede anew with Thy Heavenly Father in behalf of my poor soul, for I am of all the greatest sinner and stand in need of the greatest grace. As from the holy cross, Thou didst exclaim: "Father, forgive them for they know not what they do!"—say now in like manner for me: Father, forgive this miserable sinner, for he knows not the evil he does! As Thou didst on the cross offer Him Thy sufferings and show Him Thy wounds, offer again those bitter pains for me and show Him Thy glorious wounds. As Thou didst then appease Him perfectly, so do Thou now turn away His anger from me and obtain for me a share in His grace. Amen.

The Pater Noster with its seven petitions is here said aloud by the priest in remembrance of the Seven Last Words of Jesus on the cross.

Prayer at the Pater Noster.

O Jesus, how great was Thy love for sinners! Although they blasphemed Thee as Thou didst hang upon the cross, yet didst Thou intercede for them with Thy Father, didst promise Paradise to the penitent thief, didst recommend Thy lonely Mother to St. John, and utter those other words that revealed to the world Thy great love and sufferings! I pray Thee in virtue of those Seven Words, forgive me whatever evil I have committed by the seven deadly sins. Amen.

When before the Agnus Dei, the priest divides the Sacred Host into two parts, be mindful of Christ dying upon the cross, His blessed soul separating from His body. The particle that the priest drops into the chalice, signifies the soul of Christ descending into Limbo. After this follows the "Agnus Dei," at which both priest and people strike their breast, to signify the distress of all creatures at the death of Christ, expressed on Calvary by the Centurion who struck his breast with sincere sorrow.

Prayer before the Agnus Dei.

O martyred Jesus! By the breaking of the Sacred Host, the priest reminds us of the separation of Thy most holy soul from Thy body! O cruel, frightful, horrible death! O Jesus Christ, what superhuman tortures didst Thou not suffer in Thy death! In perfect innocence, Thou didst lay down

Thy precious life. Alas! I am the cause of Thy death! My horrible sins robbed Thee of life! Ah, by the painful separation of Thy body and soul, forgive my mortal sins, and preserve me for the future from every danger of offending Thee anew and again losing Thy grace. Amen.

Prayer at the Agnus Dei.

O innocent Lamb of God! I acknowledge my guilt before Thee and sorrowfully accuse myself of heaving caused Thy death. O most meek Lamb of God! I bewail my sins and humbly implore Thy pardon. O merciful Lamb of God! admit me again to Thy grace. Let not Thy bitter Passion and death be lost on me! O my beloved Redeemer! Thou who didst die on the cross for me, that I might live eternally, I pray Thee through Thy most bitter death to snatch me from eternal death. Offer Thy Father for my poor soul all the bitter pains Thou didst endure upon the cross, that He may remit the dire punishment my sins deserve. Amen.

The priest now says: "Domine. non sum dignus," and receives the Blessed Sacrament. This signifies the sorrowful burial of Our Lord by His holy Mother, the holy women, in union with John, Nicodemus, and Joseph of Arimathea.

Prayer at the Domine, non sum dignus.

O my Jesus, I will now call to mind how Thy dear friends, in deepest sorrow, took Thee down from the cross and bore Thee to the tomb! O that my heart were so pure as to afford Thee an abiding resting-place! Do Thou purify it, O good Jesus! Cleanse it in the rosy stream of Thine own Precious Blood, that it may become perfectly pure in Thy eyes. Adorn it with Thy virtues, enkindle in it Thy love, that it may become for Thee a worthy dwelling. O that I were worthy to partake of this sacred banquet, and to drink, were it only one drop, from this holy chalice! O sweet Jesus, with all my heart I long to receive Thee and to keep Thee always with me! As the priest now partakes of Thy flesh and blood, so, too, do I desire to participate in the same; and, by this divine remedy, to be strengthened in all good. May Thy sacred flesh feed me, Thy Precious Blood refresh me, Thy merits enrich me, and the virtue of this Holy Sacrifice obtain for me grace and mercy! Amen.

When the priest after Holy Communion, says Dominus vobiscum, think of Christ appearing to His disciples after His resurrection, saying: "Peace be with ye!"

Prayer after Holy Communion.

O glorious Jesus! Thou didst on the third day arise from the dead, and appear to Thy disciples. I rejoice in Thy glorious resurrection and congratulate Thee upon the great glory Thou didst receive from God, Thy Father. O that I, too, may be worthy to rise gloriously and rejoice forever with Thee! Ah, by the merits of Thy bitter Passion, I implore Thee to grant me this grace, that I may eternally praise Thy mercy! Amen.

The priest now gives his blessing to the people. This action is commemorative of Christ at His ascension blessing His disciples, who then went forth to proclaim the Gospel throughout the whole world.

Prayer at the Blessing.

O Blessed Jesus, Thou who, after fulfilling Thy course, didst victoriously ascend into heaven whilst with uplifted hands Thou didst bless Thy disciples, I rejoice with Thee in the great glory Thou didst then receive, and I most humbly beg Thy benediction! Extend Thy glorified hands and impart to me Thy blessing. Bless me in body and soul, and preserve me from all my enemies, visible and invisible.

Grant me also, through the power of the holy Gospel now being read, the grace to live devoutly and holily in the faithful practice of Thy divine Commandments. Amen.

When the priest says the words · Et verbum caro factum est, bow profoundly saying :

I thank Thee, O Divine Word, that Thou didst become flesh and dost dwell amongst us! Offer to God the Father the merits of Thy Sacred Humanity, and grant that I may share in the same! Amen.

Offering of the Holy Sacrifice.

O Heavenly Father, I have assisted at this Holy Mass whilst reflecting upon the Passion of Thy dear Son and sympathizing in the same. I offer to Thee my devotion, and I pray Thee to receive it graciously for the sake of Thy Divine Son. Remember, O Heavenly Father, how much Thy Only-begotten Son suffered for me, at how great a cost He purchased my soul. Ah, would it not be the greatest misfortune if all were lost on me!

My God, do not permit such an ill to befall me; but grant that I may so profit by the bitter Passion and death of Thy Divine Son as to be able to praise and glorify Thy holy Name for all eternity. Amen.

DEVOTIONS FOR CONFESSION.

It is of infinite importance to receive the holy Sacrament of Penance often and worthily. If we receive it worthily, it will infallibly obtain for us the forgiveness of all our sins and a rich increase in divine grace. But if we receive it unworthily, we commit a mortal sin and incur eternal damnation. But as we can do nothing good of ourselves, we must before confession earnestly implore the grace of God and seek to arouse in our heart a sincere desire of the divine assistance in this important affair. For this end, we will make use of the following:—

Prayer in Preparation for Confession.

O my God, urged by the inspiration of the Holy Ghost, I present myself before Thee, to receive the Sacrament of Penance, to purify my soul from sin and to adorn it anew with Thy grace! Thou knowest well, O Heavenly Father, that I cannot rightly perform this so important action, upon which the salvation of my poor soul depends, without the assistance of Thy grace. I prostrate most humbly, therefore, before the throne of Thy grace, and beg Thee, in Thy benign goodness, to help me. I cast myself at the foot of Thy holy cross also, O Lord Jesus Christ, and implore Thee, by the bitter pain Thou didst endure upon it for three long hours, to grant me the grace to receive this salutary Sacrament worthily and thus recover

Thy favor which I have lost by sin. I prostrate before Thee also, O Holy Spirit, Source of all grace, and I beg Thee to impart to me an abundance of Thy rich treasures clearly to discover my sins, heartily to bewail them, and sincerely to confess them. Amen.

Here examine your conscience, running through the Ten Commandments one after the other, and try to recall how grievously and in what way you have sinned since your last good confession. In the same manner run through the Six Commandments of the Church, the Seven Deadly Sins, and those to which you may have been accessory.

Examine yourself upon the Spiritual and Corporal Works of Mercy; for upon these especially will the Saviour question you at the judgment, to pass a favorable or an unfavorable sentence according to your fulfilment of them.

After the examination of conscience, seek to awaken in your soul true sorrow for having by your sins offended God. The foundation of true and perfect contrition is the love of God. You should, therefore, bewail your sins, because you have grieved and offended your God whom you should love more than the whole world. That a spark of that holy love may be enkindled in your heart, say the following:

Prayer to obtain True Contrition.

Father of mercy, I, Thy unworthy child, like the Prodigal Son return to Thee sincerely grieving over my sins and misdeeds. Thou art my best of Fathers. In Thy mercy, Thou hast admitted me, a poor creature, to the number of Thy children and to the inheritance of eternal goods. From the first instant of my life Thou hast, like a true Father, nourished, cherished, protected, and with paternal affection loved me. Thou hast guarded me from danger and lavished upon me innumerable favors. Had not Thy love and mercy been so great toward me, I should long ago have fallen into the abyss of hell there to burn for all eternity. For all these benefits, Thou hast never exacted from me any other return than that I should acknowledge Thy favors, thank Thee for them and, as a faithful child, serve and love Thee. But I have not done this. I have repaid Thee only with sin and ingratitude. I have not loved Thee, but experienced for Thee only coldness and indifference. I have, like a disobedient child, despised Thy Commandments; and by my many infidelities, I have afflicted Thy Divine Heart.

O my God, shall this not cause me pain? Ah, yes! That I have insulted and offended Thee, the best and highest Good, now gives me more trouble than any thing else could do! Have pity on me, O my God! Cast me not off as I have deserved. I supplicate Thee for grace and mercy. Pardon me, O my Father, pardon me and remember not my sins. With a contrite heart, I call to Thee like the Prodigal Son: "Father, I have sinned against Heaven and before Thee! I am not now worthy to be called Thy son. Make me as one of Thy hired servants!" Amen.

Prayer before Confession.

I come to Thee, my Saviour Jesus Christ, as the penitent sinner Mary Magdalen went to Thee in the house of the Pharisee, cast herself at Thy feet, wept over her sins, and confessed them to Thee as to the High-Priest. In deep humility I, too, will throw myself at the priest's feet and to him, as to Thy representative, make known my sins. Would to God that I could do it with sorrow as bitter, with tears as plentiful as did the penitent Magdalen! I offer Thee, O Jesus, the sighs and tears of all contrite hearts, to supply for my coldness and indifference. I offer Thee all the sorrow and suffering that have ever been felt by penitent hearts, and I sincerely desire to experience the same. With the most earnest longing after true and perfect contrition, I approach Thee, O my sweet Saviour, in order to cleanse my soul in Thy Precious Blood, that it may appear in Thy sight purified from every stain and adorned with Thy grace. Amen.

Having entered the confessional and recived the priest's blessing, begin your accusation with the following words:

In the spirit of humility and with a contrite heart, I confess to God, to all the saints, and to thee, Father, as the representative of God, that I have sinned in thought, word, and deed.

Here mention when you last confessed, and then accuse yourself simply and sincerely of all your sins. End your confession with the following words:

For these and all the sins of my past life, which I include, I am most heartily sorry, because I have by them offended my good God. I am resolved with the help of God never more to sin, and carefully to avoid every occasion of sin. I beg of you, Father, penance and absolution, if I am worthy of them.

Prayer whilst receiving Absolution.

O Lord Jesus Christ, Thou who didst Thyself absolve St. Magdalen from her sins, deign to absolve me from mine and to ratify in heaven the absolution that Thy priest is now pronouncing over me, that I may be loosed from sin and its punishment. Amen.

Prayer after Confession.

O my good Saviour Jesus Christ, after having confessed my sins to Thee and to Thy minister, and received absolution I have not the least doubt that Thou hast pardoned me and received me again to Thy grace. O how great are Thy love and mercy toward penitent sinners! I praise, I bless Thy goodness, and I thank Thee for having shown Thyself so loving and gracious to me. As a small satisfaction for my offences against Thee, I will now perform the penance imposed, uniting it with that immense penance which Thou didst offer for me to Thy Eternal Father in Thy bitter Passion and death. Amen.

Here perform the penance imposed, or a part of it, if it is not all to be said at once.

Offering of the Penance.

Receive, O Heavenly Father, this prayer (these prayers) that I am about to say as penance for my numerous sins. I unite it (them) with the penitential works and merits of Thy saints. Thy Son Jesus has shown Thee infinitely more love by His bitter Passion and death than I have offered Thee injury by my sins. Thy elect have rendered Thee greater and more numerous services than are the good works that I have through indifference omitted. I confide, therefore, in the merits and works of Christ and Thy saints; and I hope that Thou wilt graciously accept my penance and restore me to Thy grace, that I may never again wander from the right path. Amen.

SOME BEAUTIFUL PRAYERS FOR HOLY COMMUNION.

Among all the exercises that a pious Christian can perform for the honor of God and the forwarding of his own salvation, one of the most excellent is the worthy reception of Holy Communion. The oftener a soul receives It, the better he becomes, provided he receives with devotion and strives by means of It, daily to become more perfect. The preparation for Holy Communion, Christ Himself made known to us in these words: "Do this for a commemoration of Me."—St. Paul, also, says: "As often as you shall eat this bread and drink the chalice, you shall show the death of the Lord until He come,"—which means, as often as you receive Holy Communion, be mindful of the bitter Passion and death of Christ.

Prayer in Preparation for Holy Communion.

O Lord Jesus Christ, Son of the Living God, I am about to draw near to the most august Sacrament of the Altar and to receive Thy most sacred Flesh and Blood into my unworthy Breast. I desire to perform this holy action in such a way as will promote Thy glory, give joy to Thy saints, forward the interests of the Church, afford consolation to the poor souls in purgatory, and contribute to the salvation of my own soul. Grant me Thy grace and direct all the desires of my soul, that it may worthily prepare for the reception of

Thy Divine Majesty. I will do what in me lies, O my God, but do Thou perfect what is beyond my power! My Saviour Jesus, I implore Thee to wash my unclean heart with Thy bitter tears, to soften it with the bloody drops that fell from Thy sacred body in the sweat of death, to moisten it with the water from Thy blessed side, to sprinkle it with the rosy stream of Thy precious Blood, and to prepare in it for Thyself so lovely a dwelling-place that Thy Divine Majesty may enter therein with joy! Amen.

A Prayer Containing the Chief Points of Christ's Passion, to be said before Holy Communion.

O Lord Jesus Christ, how costly is the banquet to which Thou dost invite me, how sweet the food Thou hast prepared for me! Thou givest me Thy own sacred Body as food, Thy own sacred Blood as drink—that same blood which in Thy person is united with the Godhead and which, in Thy Passion, was so painfully poured out. Thou givest me Thy Soul, that same Soul by the Holy Ghost prepared for Thee and in Thy Passion so cruelly tormented.

Ah, what toil did it cost Thee to provide for me this food, and what pain didst Thou endure to be able to offer me this life-giving drink! Ah, Thou wast cruelly scourged, crowned with thorns, and nailed to the cross upon which Thou didst die! Thy Precious Blood was despised, was execrated, was cruelly shed. O my dear Redeemer, how afflicted wast Thou on the Mount of Olives! Thou wast, amidst scorn and derision, taken prisoner in the garden, accused falsely before the judges, rejected by the populace, scourged by the executioners, pierced with thorns, overwhelmed by the weight of the cross, fastened thereto with nails, and given over to the most cruel death. Thou wast in thy Passion abandoned by all creatures, disowned, despised, derided, blasphemed, and condemned. No one would acknowledge Thee, no one console Thee, no one give Thee refreshment, no one have compassion on Thee. Yes; Thou wast so abandoned by God and men as to be forced to cry out upon the cross: "My God, my God, why hast Thou forsaken me!"—Will no one receive Thee? Art Thou utterly abandoned, my beloved Spouse Jesus Christ? O, then, will I receive Thee as my most precious Treasure! I will compassionate Thee, my dear Saviour! Into the most secret chamber of my heart will I lead Thee, and upon the couch of my soul will I lay Thee! There will I comfort Thee, refresh Thee, console Thee, and embrace Thee! I will rest Thy wounded head upon the soft cushion of my good will; I will soothe Thy pains by my tender sympathy; I will heal Thy wounds with loving kisses; I will wash away Thy bloody stains with my tears; and instead of the innumerable outrages offered Thee in Thy Passion, I will render to Thee love and honor a thousand-fold.

O loving Mother of God, help me to prepare my soul! O my dear patrons, help me to purify my heart! O all ye holy saints, stand by me, adorn my heart with all the virtues! As you prepared your hearts to become worthy dwelling-places for the Most Holy Sacrament, so now prepare my sinful heart for the worthy reception of the same Blessed Sacrament. As you adorned your souls with all virtues, so now adorn my soul with your virtues. As you with the greatest devotion drew near to this Holy Table, so now obtain by your powerful intercession that I, too, may approach this celestial Banquet with true devotion. Beg for me true contrition for my sins, true appreciation of this Holy Sacrament, deep reverence for It, a glowing desire to receive It, my sweetest Food, so that the whole heavenly court may rejoice on beholding my devotion in receiving It. Amen.

Go with folded hands and downcast eyes to the Communion rail; kneel down and, striking your breast, say thrice:

Lord, I am not worthy that Thou shouldst enter under my roof; say but the word, and my soul shall be healed.

Then, until the moment of receiving, make use of the following aspirations of love:

O Lord Jesus Christ, I am not worthy to receive Thee! But I Trust in Thy goodness that Thou wilt not cast me away from Thee.

O Lord Jesus Christ, I am not worthy that Thou shouldst tarry with me! But I implore Thee, through the love of Thy Heart, not to despise my sinful heart. Amen.

O my Jesus, make me less unworthy! Come, O

my Love, my Supreme Good, come to me, for my soul is longing after Thee!

Prayer After Holy Communion.

Welcome, my God, my Saviour, Thou Beloved of my heart! I salute Thee, I bless Thee a thousand times! I humbly adore Thy Divinity and Thy Humanity. O my chosen Spouse, Thou art to me a fragrant nosegay of myrrh, and I will carry Thee on my breast! I press Thee to my heart in sacred love, desiring to imprint Thy holy wounds thereon. Now I have Thee truly with me, O my Redeemer, Thou who on Mount Olivet didst sweat blood for me, Thou who for me wast scourged and crowned with thorns, Thou who wast fastened to the cross and upon it didst yield Thy last sigh! Thou, my well-beloved Jesus, I now possess, Thou who wast, out of love for me, so wounded from head to foot that there was no part of Thy body that did not suffer its special pain. To assuage Thy sufferings and to make Thee some returns for the outrages offered Thee, I have received Thee into my heart; and I desire to give Thee a thousand times more love and honor than in Thy bitter Passion Thou didst endure scorn and pain. Thy thorn-crowned head, I rest upon my penitent heart, to soothe its throbbing pains. Thy lacerated body I lay in the bosom of my soul as on a downy couch, that there Thou mayst sweetly slumber and forget the weary past. The gaping wounds of Thy hands and feet I will bedew with tears from my eyes, to heal them in that bath of sorrow and free them from their pains. On Thy pallid lips, let me impress the sweetest kiss of love, as a sign of what glows in my heart for Thee. O my chosen Spouse, may this, my good will, be pleasing to Thee! Accept these poor services that I offer Thee in spirit, as if it had indeed been my blessed privilege to bestow them really at the time of Thy Passion.

Since I possess Thee, my Crucified Saviour, in my heart, allow me to treat Thee with that confidence that my love dictates. Let Thy wounded head subdue the pride of mine, Thy disfigured countenance efface the sins of mine, Thy wan lips atone for the offences of mine, Thy pierced hands satisfy for the misdeeds of mine, Thy nailed feet obtain pardon for the wicked ways in which mine have wandered, Thy wounded body obtain for me pardon for all the sins of mine, Thy pierced Heart heal the wounds of my sinful heart, Thy streaming Blood wash my soul clean of every stain, Thy painful Passion pay off all my debts, and Thy bitter death secure for me eternal life! Amen.

Thanksgiving and Offering after Holy Communion.

What return can I make to Thee, O my Jesus, for the great grace Thou hast shown me? As I am wholly unable to comprehend the happiness that is mine in Holy Communion, so neither am I able to make any return to Thee for the same; therefore, I beg all the angels and saints of heaven to help me praise and thank Thee worthily for all Thy benefits.

As all devout souls have ever thanked Thee after Holy Communion, so also do I desire with all my strength to thank Thee and to make some return for the infinite love which Thou hast shown me. I pray Thee, O my Jesus, not to leave me without imparting to me Thy blessing and wounding my heart with Thy bitter Passion, that I may truly experience in my soul what Thou didst endure in Thy afflicted soul. Forgive me all the faults and negligence that I may have committed in my preparation for this Holy Communion, in my actual reception of it, and those of which I am now guilty in my thanksgiving. Ah, let not the virtue and effects of the Sacrament be hindered by them! I pray also, sweet Jesus, for the salvation of all those that have recommended themselves to my prayers, as well as of those for whom I am bound to pray. Thou knowest the names and the wants of those for whom I pray. Help them in their needs, strengthen them in their weakness, console them in their sorrows, and preserve them in Thy grace. Deliver the souls of the departed, especially those for whom I am bound to pray, from their heavy punishment and, by the power of this Most Blessed Sacrament, lead them to eternal joy and peace. Amen.

LITANY OF THE BLESSED VIRGIN,

Commonly called the Litany of Loretto.

(Translation taken from "The Raccolta," New Edition.)

Kyrie eleison,	Lord, have mercy.
Christe eleison.	Christ, have mercy.
Kyrie eleison.	Lord, have mercy.
Christe, audi nos.	Christ, hear us.
Christe, exaudi nos.	Christ, graciously hear us.
Pater de coelis Deus, miserere nobis.	God, the Father of heaven, have mercy on us.
Fili Redemptor mundi Deus, miserere nobis.	God, the Son, Redeemer of the world, have mercy on us.
Spiritus Sancte Deus, miserere nobis.	God, the Holy Ghost, have mercy on us.
Sancta Trinitas, unus Deus, miserere nobis.	Holy Trinity, one God, have mercy on us.

Latin (*Ora pro nobis.*)	English (*Pray for us.*)
Sancta Maria,	Holy Mary,
Sancta Dei Genitrix,	Holy Mother of God,
Sancta virgo virginum,	Holy Virgin of virgins,
Mater Christi,	Mother of Christ,
Mater divinae gratiae,	Mother of divine grace,
Mater purissima,	Mother most pure,
Mater castissima,	Mother most chaste,
Mater inviolata,	Mother inviolate.
Mater intemerata,	Mother undefiled,
Mater amabilis,	Mother most amiable,
Mater admirabilis,	Mother most admirable,
Mater Creatoris,	Mother of our Creator,
Mater Salvatoris.	Mother of our Saviour,
Virgo prudentissima,	Virgin most prudent.
Virgo veneranda,	Virgin most venerable,
Virgo praedicanda.	Virgin most renowned,
Virgo potens,	Virgin most powerful,
Virgo clemens,	Virgin most merciful,
Virgo fidelis,	Virgin most faithful,
Speculum justitiæ,	Mirror of justice.
Sedes sapientiae,	Seat of wisdom,
Causa nostrae laetitiae,	Cause of our joy,
Vas spirituale,	Spiritual vessel,
Vas honorabile,	Vessel of honor,

Vas insigne devotionis,	Singular vessel of devotion,
Rosa mystica,	Mystical rose,
Turris Davidica,	Tower of David,
Turris eburnea,	Tower of ivory,
Domus aurea,	House of gold,
Foederis arca,	Ark of the Covenant,
Janua coeli,	Gate of heaven,
Stella matutina,	Morning star,
Salus infirmorum,	Health of the sick,
Refugium peccatorum,	Refuge of sinners,
Consolatrix afflictorum,	Comforter of the afflicted,
Auxilium Christianorum,	Help of Christians,
Regina angelorum,	Queen of angels,
Regina patriarcharum,	Queen of patriarchs,
Regina prophetarum,	Queen of prophets,
Regina apostolorum,	Queen of Apostles,
Regina martyrum,	Queen of martyrs,
Regina confessorum,	Queen of confessors,
Regina virginum,	Queen of virgins,
Regina sanctorum omnium,	Queen of all saints,
Regina sine labe originali concepta,	Queen conceived without original sin,
Regina sacratissimi Rosarii,*	Queen of the most holy Rosary,
Regina sacratissimi Rosarii,	Queen of the most Holy Rosary.

(center: *Ora pro nobis.* — right: *Pray for us.*)

Agnus Dei, qui tollis peccata mundi, parce nobis, Domine.
Lamb of God, who takest away the sins of the world, spare us, O Lord!

Agnus Dei, qui tollis peccata mundi, exaudi nos, Domine,
Lamb of God, who takest away the sins of the world, graciously hear us, O Lord!

Agnus Dei, qui tollis peccata mundi, miserere nobis.
Lamb of God, who takest away the sins of the world, have mercy on us.

Christe, audi nos! Christ, hear us!
Christe, exaudi nos! Christ, graciously hear us!
Kyrie eleison. Lord, have mercy on us.
Christe eleison. Christ, have mercy on us.
Kyrie eleison. Lord, have mercy on us.
Pater noster. Ave Maria. Our Father. Hail Mary.

---

*The repetition of this invocation, prescribed by Leo XIII., Dec. 24, 1883, to the whole Church, is here set down merely for the confraternities of the Rosary and other Sodalities.

Ant. Sub tuum praesidium confugimus, Sancta Dei Genitrix. Nostras deprecationes ne despicias in necessitatibus, sed a periculis cunctis libera nos semper, Virgo gloriosa et benedicta.

V. Ora pro nobis, sancta Dei Genitrix.

R. Ut digni efficiamur promissionibus Christi.

Oremus.

Gratiam tuam, quaesumus Domine, mentibus nostris infunde: ut qui, angelo nuntiante, Christi Filii tui incarnationem cognovimus, per passionem ejus et crucem ad resurrectionis gloriam perducamur. Per eumdem Christum Dominum nostrum.

R. Amen.

Ant. We fly to thy patronage, O holy Mother of God. Despise not our petitions in our necessities, but deliver us from all danger, O ever glorious and blessed Virgin.

V. Pray for us, O holy Mother of God.

R. That we may be made worthy of the promises of Christ.

Let us pray.

Pour forth, we beseech Thee, O Lord, Thy grace into our hearts, that we to whom the incarnation of Christ, Thy Son, was made known by the message of an angel, may, by His passion and cross, be brought to the glory of His resurrection. Through the same Christ, our Lord.

R. Amen.

Prayer to Jesus Crucified.

(Translation from " The Raccolta," New Edition.)

Look down upon me, good and gentle Jesus, while before Thy face I humbly kneel and with burning soul pray and beseech Thee to fix deep in my heart lively sentiments of faith, hope, and charity, true contrition for my sins, and a firm purpose of amendment; the while I contemplate with great love and tender pity Thy five wounds, pondering over them within me, whilst I call to mind the words which David, Thy prophet, said of Thee, my Jesus: "They have pierced my hands and my feet; they have numbered all my bones." (Ps. xxi., 17-18.)

Whoever recites this prayer, with contrition and devotion before a Crucifix after confession and Holy Communion, can gain a Plenary indulgence applicable to the poor souls in purgatory.

An Offering.

To be made during Holy Mass, either at the Offertory, or directly after the Consecration, or before the priest's Communion.

Eternal Father, I offer Thee the sacrifice which Thy beloved Son Jesus made of Himself on the cross and now renews on this altar. I offer it in the name of all creatures together with the Masses that have been said and that will be said, throughout the whole world, to adore Thee and to give Thee the honor which Thou deservest; to render to Thee the thanks that are due Thee for Thy numberless benefits, to appease Thy anger, and to satisfy for our many sins; to supplicate Thee for myself, for the Church, for the whole world, and for the blessed souls in purgatory.

His Holiness, Pope Pius IX., granted an Indulgence of *three years*, once a day, to all that shall recite the foregoing prayer in the morning. The same Indulgence, once a day, to all that shall say it devoutly at Mass. To all that shall say it daily for a month, a Plenary Indulgence, applicable to the souls in purgatory, to be gained on the usual conditions of praying for the Church, &c.

Seven Offerings of the Precious Blood of Jesus to be said during Holy Mass or at the Visit to the Blessed Sacrament.

I. Eternal Father! I offer Thee the merit of the Precious Blood of Jesus, Thy well-beloved Son, my Saviour, and my God, for my dear Mother, the Holy Church, that she may enlarge her borders and be magnified in all the nations of the earth; for the safety and well-being of her visible head, the Sovereign Roman Pontiff; for the cardinals, bishops, and pastors of souls, and for all the ministers of Thy sanctuary.

Glory to the Father, &c.

Eternal praise and thanksgiving to Jesus, who has redeemed us with His Precious Blood!

II. Eternal Father, I offer Thee the merit of the Precious Blood of Jesus, Thy well-beloved Son, my Saviour and my God, for peace and union among all Catholic kings and princes, for the humbling of the enemies of our holy faith, and for the welfare of all Christian people.

Glory be to the Father, &c.

Eternal praise and thanksgiving to Jesus, &c.

III. Eternal Father, I offer Thee the merit of the Precious Blood of Jesus, Thy well-beloved Son, my Saviour and my God, for the repentance of unbelievers, for the uprooting of heresy, and for the conversion of sinners.

Glory be to the Father, &c.

Eternal praise and thanksgiving to Jesus, &c.

IV. Eternal Father, I offer Thee the merit of the Precious Blood of Jesus, Thy well-beloved Son, my Saviour and my God, for all my kindred friends, and enemies; for the poor, the sick, the wretched, and for all for whom Thou, my God, knowest that I ought to pray, or wouldst have me pray.

    Glory be to the Father, &c.
Eternal praise and thanksgiving to Jesus, &c.

V. Eternal Father, I offer Thee the merit of the Precious Blood of Jesus, Thy well-beloved Son, my Saviour and my God, for all that are this day passing to another life; that Thou wouldst save them from the pains of hell, and admit them quickly to the possession of Thy glory.

    Glory be to the Father, &c.
Eternal praise and thanksgiving to Jesus, &c.

VI. Eternal Father, I offer Thee the merit of the Precious Blood of Jesus, Thy well-beloved Son, my Saviour and my God, for all those that love this great treasure, for those that join with me in adoring and honoring it, and for all that spread devotion to it.

    Glory be to the Father, &c.
Eternal praise and thanksgiving to Jesus, &c.

VII. Eternal Father, I offer Thee the merit of the Precious Blood of Jesus, Thy well-beloved Son, my Saviour and my God, for all my wants, spiritual and temporal, in aid of the holy souls in purgatory, and chiefly for those that most loved this Blood, the price of our Redemption, and for those that were most devout to the sorrows and pains of most holy Mary, our dear Mother.

Glory be to the Father, &c.
Eternal praise and thanksgiving to Jesus, &c.
Glory be to the Blood of Jesus now and forever and ever. Amen.

Pope Pius VII. granted to all that would make these offerings with devotion and with the intention thereby to make compensation for the outrages offered the Precious Blood of Jesus, an Indulgence of 300 days for each recital. To all that make these offerings daily for a month, a Plenary Indulgence on any day at option after confession and Communion, provided they pray for the intentions of the Sovereign Pontiff.

(From the "Raccolta." New edition.)

Prayer of St. Francis Xavier for the Conversion of Unbelievers.

Eternal God, Creator of all things, remember that Thou didst create the souls of infidels, framing them to Thy own image and likeness. Behold, O Lord, how to Thy dishonor hell is daily replenished with them. Remember, O Lord, Thy only Son, Jesus Christ, who suffered for them, most bountifully shedding His Precious Blood. Suffer not, O Lord, Thy Son and our Lord to be any longer despised by infidels; but rather, being appeased by the entreaties and prayers of the elect, the saints, and of the Church, the most blessed spouse of Thy Son, vouchsafe to be mindful of Thy mercy, and forgetting their idolatry and infidelity, cause them also to know Him whom Thou didst send, Jesus Christ, Thy Son, our Lord, who is our health, life, and resurrection, through whom we are made free and saved, to whom be all glory forever. Amen.

Indulgence of 300 days for every recital. Rescript of Pope Pius IX. May 24, 1847.

Translation from "Raccolta," New Ed.

Daily Prayer for all that are to die during the next twenty-four hours.

O clementissime Jesu, amator animarum, obsecro te per agoniam Cordis tui sacratissimi per dolores matris tuae immaculatae, lava in sanguine tuo peccatores totius mundi, nunc positos in agonia et hodie morituros. Amen.

Cor Jesu, in agonia factum, miserere morientium!

Most merciful Jesus, Lover of souls! I pray Thee by the agony of Thy most sacred Heart and the sorrows of Thy Immaculate Mother, wash in Thy Blood the sinners of the whole world who are now in their agony and are to die this day. Amen.

Agonizing Heart of Jesus, have pity on the dying.

Indulgence of 100 days for each recital. To all that shall say it at least three times a day for a month, at different hours of the day, a Plenary Indulgence, once a month, on any day when, after confession and Communion, they shall visit a church or public oratory and there pray for some time for the intention of His Holiness. Applicable to the souls in purgatory. Decree of Feb. 2, 1850.

(From "Raccolta," New Edition.)

Act of Reparation to the Most Blessed Sacrament. *

Jesus, my God, my Saviour, with that lowly homage with which faith inspires me, I worship Thee, true God and true man! With my whole heart, I love Thee enclosed in the most august Sacrament of the altar, in reparation for all the acts of irreverence, profanation, and sacrilege, which, to my shame, I may ever have committed, as well as for all those which have ever been committed, or may ever be committed in ages yet to come.

I adore Thee, my God, not indeed as much as Thou deservest, or as much as I ought, but according to the little strength I have; and I would fain adore Thee with all the perfection of every rational creature. Meantime, 1 purpose now, and forever, to adore Thee not only for those Catholics that adore Thee not, and love Thee not, but also for the conversion of all heretics, schismatics, Mahometans, Jews, blasphemers, idolaters, and wicked Christians. Ah, my Jesus, may all men ever know, adore, love, and praise Thee every moment in the most holy and most divine Sacrament! Amen.

Pope Leo XII. granted an Indulgence of 200 days, applicable to the souls in purgatory, to all the faithful for the devout recital of this act before the Most Blessed Sacrament.

---

* By Very Rev. Humbert, Fifth General of the Dominican Order.

The Heroic Act of Charity.

O my God! in union with the merits of Jesus and Mary, I offer Thee in behalf of the poor souls in purgatory all my own satisfactory works and those of all others that shall be applied to me in life, in death, and after my passage to eternity. Amen.

By the Decree, "Urbis et Orbis," of Sept. 30, 1852, Pope Pius IX. granted to all that shall make the foregoing Act, the following Indulgences:

1. For priests, any altar whatsoever upon which they shall celebrate the Sacred Mysteries, is privileged for every Mass;

2. To the faithful a Plenary Indulgence at every Communion they receive, and upon every Monday for simply assisting at the Holy Sacrifice for the poor souls, even without going to Holy Communion.

In both these cases, they must visit a church and there pray for the intentions of the Pope.

3. He that has made this Heroic Act, may apply to the souls all the Indulgences he can gain, although such application be not expressed in the formula of concession.

Laus Patri sit ac Genito
Simulque sancto Flamini,
Qui Sancti Thomae merito
Nos coeli jungat agmini.
Amen.

Praise to the Father and the Son!
Praise to the Spirit, Three in One!
St. Thomas, help? Obtain that we
'Mongst hosts celestial ranked may be.
Amen.

INDEX.

Preface.. 1
Dedication 3
Introduction 5

Considerations for the Six Sundays Preceding the Feast of St. Thomas of Aquin.

Consideration for the First Sunday.................... 9
Prayer 16
Trait from the Life of St. Thomas of Aquin............ 17
Consideration for the Second Sunday.................. 19
Prayer.. 26
Trait from the Life of St. Thomas...................... 27
Consideration for the Third Sunday.................... 30
Prayer.. 37
Trait from the Life of St. Thomas...................... 38
Consideration for the Fourth Sunday.................. 40
Prayer.. 46
Trait from the Life of St. Thomas...................... 48
Consideration for the Fifth Sunday.................... 49
Prayer 56
Trait from the Life of St. Thomas...................... 58
Consideration for the Sixth Sunday.................... 59
Prayer.. 66
Trait from the Life of St. Thomas...................... 68
The Angelic Militia, or The Confraternity of the Cord of St. Thomas....................................... 70
Indulgences attached to the Angelic Militia........... 74
Conditions attached to Membership.................... 76
Indulgenced Prayer for the Members................... 77

Hymns of St. Thomas to the Most Blessed Sacrament.

Lauda Sion... 79
Translation 81
Sacris Solemniis.. 83
Translation 84
Verbum Supernum....................................... 85
Translation 85
Pange Lingua... 86
Translation... 87
Adoro Te... 88
Translation 89

Prayers of St. Thomas of Aquin.

Prayer for the Preservation of Chastity	91
Prayer before Holy Communion	91
Prayer after Holy Communion	92
Prayer to the Blessed Virgin Mary	93
Prayer of St. Thomas before study, &c	95
Short Prayer which St. Thomas daily said kneeling	96
Daily Prayer of St. Thomas to obtain a Holy Life	96
Prayer of St. Thomas to obtain the Virtues	98
Letter of St. Thomas to a Novice	100
Crux Angelica	101

The Daily Exercises of a Christian

Morning Prayers	103
Evening Prayers	107
Prayers at Mass	110
Devotions for Confession	126
Devotions for Holy Communion	131
Litany of the Blessed Virgin	138

Some Indulgenced Prayers.

Prayer to Jesus Crucified	140
An Offering for Holy Mass	141
Seven Offerings of the Precious Blood of Jesus	142
Prayer of St. Francis Xavier	144
Daily Prayer for the Agonizing	145
Act of Reparation to the Most Blessed Sacrament	146
The Heroic Act of Charity	147

www.ingramcontent.com/pod-product-compliance
Lightning Source LLC
Chambersburg PA
CBHW030346170426
43202CB00010B/1264